SPEAKER'S CORNER is a provocative series designed to stimulate, educate, and foster discussion on significant public policy topics. Written by experts in a variety of fields, these brief and engaging books should be read by anyone interested in the trends and issues that shape our world.

IRAQ
UNCENSORED

Perspectives

Edited by Dr. James M. Ludes
AMERICAN SECURITY PROJECT
Foreword by Senator John Kerry

FULCRUM
GOLDEN, COLORADO

Library of Congress Cataloging-in-Publication Data

Iraq uncensored : perspectives / American Security Project ; edited by James M. Ludes.
    p. cm. -- (Speaker's corner)
  ISBN 978-1-55591-703-6 (hardcover)
  1. Iraq War, 2003- 2. Iraq War, 2003---Influence. 3. National security--United States. 4. Military policy--United States. I. Ludes, James M. II. American Security Project.
  DS79.76.I72715 2009
  956.7044'3--dc22
                       2009011509

Printed on recycled paper in Canada by Friesens Corp.
0 9 8 7 6 5 4 3 2 1

Cover image © Gary Paul Lewis | Shutterstock

Fulcrum Publishing
4690 Table Mountain Drive, Suite 100
Golden, Colorado 80403
800-992-2908 • 303-277-1623
www.fulcrumbooks.com

TO THOSE WHO SERVE

CONTENTS

ACKNOWLEDGMENTS

This book is the sum of its parts. The authors deserve every credit for their insightful contributions. To my colleagues at the American Security Project, especially Amy Gergely, who worked tirelessly on early drafts of many of these essays, Bernard Finel, Holly Gell, Selena Shilad, and Christine Dehn, I owe a special debt of gratitude. Any failures in this volume, however, are mine.

I also want to thank my family and friends for putting up with me and my generally overbooked schedule. A special debt of gratitude is reserved for Anne, who inspires me in profound ways, and for my parents, Elaine and Jake, who make everything possible.

FOREWORD

Senator John Kerry

No war is easy. Combat is never simple. But Iraq in particular has failed to submit itself to even relatively simple or easy shorthand.

Just think, in the last six years Iraq has been many things to many people, some seemingly contradictory: a failure of diplomacy to keep weapons of mass destruction out of the hands of a dictator; a preemptive war to achieve what diplomacy was not given the time to accomplish; a demonstration of the brilliance of American troops; a failure to listen to generals and State Department experts about what would come next; an ideological overreach to transform an entire region; a massive intelligence failure; an insurgency, teetering on the brink of sectarian civil war; the start and stop and start again of reluctant civil institutions; a Sunni awakening complemented by a new military and political strategy; an orderly redeployment of troops leaving Iraqis largely responsible for their own future.

All this and more—the good, the bad, the ugly— the layers of policy to be dissected and debated from

America's war of choice in what was once called the cradle of civilization will occupy historians for generations.

And the last chapter is now largely in Iraqi hands.

Yes, war has been with us since the dawn of man. Our efforts—our dreams—of making it less common have been frustrated time and again. Institutions, treaties, and theories advancing this cause have all collapsed under the weight of history.

But even by that standard, Iraq is different. Seldom have the conventional definitions of foreign policy positions been turned on their heads so much as they were in this war.

It may be too early to draw definite conclusions about the Iraq war, but it is not too early to begin asking the question. This effort by the American Security Project is among the first to ask a broad cross section of observers: What should we learn from the Iraq war?

The purpose is not to pave the way for more Iraqs or to find some convenient new theory to prevent the next Iraq, but to learn from this experience so that we, as a nation, may gain wisdom, not simply to fight some future war better—but to learn valuable lessons about people and human events so that we can advance the cause of freedom and security, peace and justice, and so that we will be better equipped to be an America that only goes to war because it has to, never because we "want to."

Iraq Uncensored begins a dialogue about the lessons of the Iraq war that will last for decades. No matter what you believe about the war—its wisdom, its purpose, or its cost—it is every American's duty to at least grapple with the issues raised by it. Whether we admit it or not, the Iraq experience will shade, for good or for bad, the foreign policy debate for years to come. We are better off acknowledging that fact head-on than ignoring it as inconvenient or thinking we can hit the reset button for foreign policy.

Some authors will disagree with each other on the lessons, and so will readers. This isn't easy. But no war is. And that's the point.

INTRODUCTION

James M. Ludes

Over the course of eighteen months, the American Security Project put the following question to some of the most creative minds in national security: What is the single most important lesson the United States should learn from the war in Iraq?

The answers we received are published in the pages that follow. They are neither pro-war nor antiwar. They run the gamut from how to better approach similar operations to pleas to never undertake such missions again. Each response reflects the unique perspective of its author. Collectively, they reveal a greater diversity of opinion on the war in Iraq than can be found in recent public-opinion surveys on the topic. While the public has rejected the strategic utility of the war, there are many analysts who continue to focus on what might have been done differently at the tactical level.

At best, we can conclude that the Iraq war remains a divisive issue in America. Any effort to draw lessons from the war risks becoming bogged down in partisan debate about the way the Bush administration led the country to war. But a discussion of this importance cannot be dismissed as partisan grandstanding. This is a conversation we must have as a nation. For the truth is that historians will spend decades examining this conflict, its causes, its conduct, and its consequences. In the meantime, we face an urgency to learn from the experience so that any new decisions about war and peace are better informed, more thoroughly vetted, and more rationally made.

In the first section, The Coming of the War, Paul Pillar and Bishop John Bryson Chane reflect on the war from inside the intelligence community and inside the peace movement, respectively. Robert Gallucci looks at the case for war and concludes that in the future, the United States should only go to war when compelling reasons can be articulated by the administration and withstand examination by Congress and the American people.

In Part Two, The Conduct of the War, Lt. Gen. Daniel Christman discusses the mismatch between American objectives in Iraq and the resources dedicated to the effort. Robert Hormats laments the lack of an effective political-military strategy. Steven Livingston examines the failures of American journalists, while V. Adm. Lee F. Gunn applies lessons from other eras to America's desire to depart Iraq now. John Nagl and Bernard Finel come to different conclusions about the comparison of Vietnam to Iraq, and Thomas P. M. Barnett looks at the lessons the rest of the world might draw from America's war in Iraq.

In Part Three, the discussion shifts to issues of strategy. Arthur Obermayer provides insights about irregular warfare while Brig. Gen. Steve Cheney, Joseph Collins, and Morton Halperin describe the need to broaden the capacity of the American government to operate more effectively—beyond the Department of Defense—in future crises and war zones. Shibley Telhami, in contrast, warns of the dangers of dismantling nation states. Finally, Benjamin Friedman and Christopher Preble warn that the principle lesson of Iraq should be to avoid similar wars in the future.

In Part Four, Adm. Bill Owens dives into the business of defense. Gordon Adams unmasks the damage done to the Pentagon's budget system by the off-budget funding of the war. Lawrence Korb describes the harm inflicted on the all-volunteer army. Lt. Gen. Claudia Kennedy, the first woman to achieve that rank in the history of the United States Army, notes the performance of women on the battlefield. And Frank Hoffman, a marine and a scholar, urges greater involvement by America's political leaders in the development and execution of strategy.

In the final section of the book, former senator Gary Hart reminds readers that the United States is a republic—a form of political organization that imbues citizens with responsibilities and puts real constraints on the policies we can sustain. And Jim Miller examines what "No More Iraqs" really means.

Taken together, these essays are the start of a dialogue, not just about Iraq, but about America's role in the world. The world we seek, the challenges we confront, and the means we use to further our interests are vital issues that every American should consider. In the pages that follow, the debate begins. We hope you will continue it long after you turn the final page.

PART ONE
The Coming of the War

Informed Decisions: Process before Policy

Paul R. Pillar

How we draw lessons from the experience in Iraq is important and itself reflects on the lessons of the Iraq experience. The substantive issues raised by the war—ranging from the utility of military force to principles of counterinsurgency, prospects for democratization, trends in Middle Eastern politics, and much else—are so numerous and complex that it is difficult to avoid drawing wrong lessons along with the right ones.

In any future situation in which one might hope to apply the lessons learned painfully in Iraq, it will be essential to assess that situation carefully to identify how it may differ from, as well as resemble, Iraq. The process of assessment must consider all the relevant variables that can affect US interests, all the possible ways of pursuing US objectives and the pros and cons of each way, and all the things that could go wrong, as well as their likelihood of going wrong.

The implication of this is not that we should prejudge the results of any one assessment. Instead, it is to ensure that such assessments are made and that they are fully applied to, and reflected in, decisions on foreign policy.

That brings us to the most egregious shortcoming

exhibited in the Iraq episode, one that underlies the entire ill-fated expedition and thus underlies so many other specific problems and potential lessons to be learned: there was no process that used the resources and perspectives in the executive branch of the government (nor tapped available expertise outside government) to consider whether or not to launch the war.

It is not that there was a defective process—there was *no* process. There was no meeting, no options paper, and no other forum in which basic considerations and arguments about whether or not to invade Iraq were ever examined. There was much discussion inside the executive branch aimed at selling the decision to invade, and some also at implementing the decision, but not at making the decision in the first place.

At least that is what we know based on the record to date, including the first draft of history that journalists have written. If there were any discussions about the actual decision to go to war, they were confined to the most impenetrable private conversations of the president, vice president, and conceivably a few others. For future historians who will write subsequent drafts, the most astounding thing about this momentous initiative—launching America's first major offensive war in over a century—will be that the Bush administration took it without ever first examining systematically whether it was a good idea.

The absence of any process for vetting the war decision meant that a host of important considerations were never brought to bear on that decision. Especially important among those considerations were the many challenges and ramifications of trying to pacify, reconstruct, and politically transform Iraq. The absence of a process meant that even when parts of the bureaucracy had insights and input to offer, there usually was no audience for those inputs. And it meant that with no clear line between pre- and post-decision phases of the lead-up to war, the line between professional responsibility and insubordination also became blurred. Offering candid, even if unsolicited, advice to decision makers is appropriate behavior before a decision is made; saluting and pursuing the mission is most appropriate after the fact.

The absence of a policy process within the administration was part of a larger deficiency, involving Congress, the press, and the public, in failing to examine carefully and critically everything that should have been examined before endorsing the war. What passed for a debate was largely confined to the administration's selling points of weapons of mass destruction and terrorist links, with huge unfilled gaps in logic between premises contained in the sales campaign and any conclusion that an invasion was advisable. There are other lessons to be learned from the deficiencies in that debate, although some of what transpired reflects inherent weaknesses of a democracy making foreign policy. But the starting point for the deficiencies that followed was the absence of debate within the administration itself.

So the single biggest lesson of Iraq is: have a policymaking process. Before making a major foreign-policy decision, much less selling it to the public or implementing it, engage every relevant department and agency in a thorough examination of all of the national interests at stake and all of the ways in which different possible courses of action will affect those interests.

The executive branch is no stranger to such processes. Although each new administration tweaks the interdepartmental machinery for making national security policy, there are well-established procedures for reviewing and debating policy options as part of preparing an issue for decision by the president, even though those procedures were conspicuously absent in the case of Iraq. The question is not one of thinking up new procedures, but rather of willingness to use them consistently.

There is no good way for outsiders to enforce such consistency, beyond asking tough questions about how decisions were made. Each president gets the policymaking procedures that he or she wants. It is future presidents, therefore, who need to absorb this particular lesson. Absorption may depend on those future presidents realizing that pursuit of even the most principled objectives may have flaws, and that even bureaucracies—annoying as they sometimes seem—may have something useful to say in pointing out both flaws and opportunities.

A Very Bad Idea from the Start

Robert Gallucci

The United States launched a military operation against Iraq without a compelling reason for doing so. We may have learned a lot from our many mistakes after the end of large-unit military operations and the fall of Baghdad, but a larger lesson should be drawn from the decision to invade Iraq in the first place. This was not a good idea badly executed; it was a very bad idea from the start.

Much has been made of the failure of the intelligence community to correctly characterize Iraq's capability with respect to weapons of mass destruction—chemical, biological, and nuclear. And, in fact, the intelligence assessment did mistakenly have Iraq in possession of chemical and biological weapons. But it *did not* assert that Iraq had nuclear weapons, only that it could build such weapons more quickly than other countries—if it were to acquire the necessary fissile material—because it had done essential research and development before the first Gulf War.

This is not a fine point; it is a fundamental one. The administration never explained how it presumed biological and chemical weapons threatened the United States or its allies, where Iraq would acquire sufficient fissile material to build a militarily significant nuclear capability, or why the United States' overwhelming conventional and nuclear forces could not deter Iraq from acting against American interests and its friends in the Middle East.

There were, to be sure, suggestions from the policy community that Iraq was connected with terrorists and even to those responsible for the attacks of September 11, 2001. But the intelligence community did not support those claims.

Iraq did not attack anyone in 2003, nor was it about to attack anyone. At best, the United States launched a preventive war without sufficient evidence that America's vital interests would ever be put at risk by Iraq. At best, we were responding to Iraq's flagrant violation of numerous United Nations Security Council Resolutions, without the support of the international community. At best, we miscalculated and overreached.

At worst, we went to war, invaded a country, and overthrew a government in order to shape the political landscape of a region more to our liking, not to stop aggression or to defend vital interests. Nor was this an intervention launched for humanitarian reasons, to free the Iraqi people from Saddam Hussein's oppression. This was not an essential part of the argument—at least not before the invasion.

The lesson, then, from our experience in Iraq is that the United States should go to war only when there are compelling reasons to do so, reasons that can be articulated by the government and stand up to the scrutiny of the Congress and the people.

Real Faith in the Public Square

John Bryson Chane

In his book *The Culture of Disbelief: How American Law and Politics Trivialize Religious Devotion*, Yale law professor Dr. Stephen Carter expressed the concerns of many about the negative impact of religious power when it mixes too intimately with political power. His writing reveals one of the great tragedies that preceded the Bush administration's push to engage in a preemptive war with Iraq in 2003. Carter wrote:

> But the greater threat comes when the church is no longer kept merely separate but is forced into a position of utter subservience, its voice disregarded in the greater public discussions or even disqualified from joining them. The real danger is that citizens in general will accept the culture's assumption that religious faith has no real bearing on civic responsibility. Should that happen, prevailing cultural mores will have a higher claim on us than do privately held convictions of conscience, however arrived at. When faith is removed from public life, when we divorce religion from politics, we marginalize religion to the point that the values that

ultimately guide and help society behave in a reasonable and compassionate fashion are lost to the current and prevailing values of the culture.

There is little doubt that the administration did all in its power to co-opt the leadership of all the mainline religious denominations in the United States to support its invasion plans to remove Saddam Hussein from power and to impart a distorted version of Western democracy to that country. The administration believed that success in Iraq would breed success in other Islamic Middle Eastern countries considered to be hostile or antithetical to American interests. The neoconservative political movement that was the driving force behind American foreign policy—especially during the first four years of George W. Bush's presidency—led the American people to believe that there was a clear connection between the terrorist attacks of September 11, 2001, and Iraq. To press that point and to build on the fear of the American people generated by these attacks on American soil, the administration believed it was critical for the broad base of American faith communities to weigh in, support a preemptive strike against Iraq, and by doing so lend credibility to the administration's actions.

In the autumn of 2002, I received an invitation from Secretary of Defense Rumsfeld to attend a briefing with a small number of religious leaders from the United States at the Pentagon. The briefing packet I received prior to the meeting outlined US military strategy currently in place in Afghanistan. The invitation came at a time when I had been the bishop of Washington for only a few short months and the opportunity to discuss matters concerning our foreign policy in the Middle East with both Secretary Rumsfeld and Paul Wolfowitz, the deputy secretary of defense, was an invitation I couldn't refuse. As one who opposed any further military incursion into the Middle East beyond Afghanistan, I had become increasingly concerned with the administration's rhetoric about Iraq and the accusations that Iraq possessed weapons of mass destruction.

The administration's war drums were beginning to beat loudly in November 2002 to engage in military action against Iraq on the theory that such military action would remove the much-hated dictator Saddam Hussein from power and would also reduce the threat of terrorism directed against the United States. I viewed the invitation to attend the Pentagon meeting as an opportunity to express my point of view as a religious leader that such an incursion into Iraq, instead of decreasing the threat of terrorism, would act as a major recruiting tool for a whole new wave of well-trained terrorists who would increase the likelihood of further attempts to do harm to Western governments, their citizens, and institutions. I was also concerned that to shift our focus from the Taliban and to engage in a military operation against Iraq would weaken our military presence in Afghanistan. Such a move would strengthen the hand of the Taliban at a time when significant progress by American military forces had been achieved in routing them from their brutal control of that country.

It was also my belief, a belief shared by many others at the time, that real energy needed to be generated by the administration to take an active leadership role in effectively putting into place the "Road Map for Peace" between Israel and Palestine. It was no secret that many Arab countries viewed Israel's incursions into Palestinian territory, and blatant disregard for United Nations Resolutions prohibiting such action, as the cause of great concern in the Middle East. The United States needed to be responsive in pushing forward the road map in the eyes of most Arab nations. For them this was a first-order priority that needed the leadership of both the United States and Great Britain.

At the November Pentagon meeting, the conversation led by Wolfowitz and Rumsfeld switched quickly from Afghanistan to Iraq. The switch appeared to be no accident given the increased media coverage on Iraq and the fact that religious leaders including my own presiding bishop of the Episcopal Church, the Most Reverend Frank Griswold, were present. "Shock and awe" as a strategy was placed on the table for discussion for the first time and to me appeared as a craftily designed program of three days of highly technical, precisely pinpointed heavy bombardment of the Iraqi army and the command centers of Hussein that, according to Rumsfeld, would force the Iraqi military to surrender en masse and lay down its arms. Collateral damage would be minimal in such an engagement and civilian casualties could be kept very low. Invading American forces would ultimately be welcomed by the Iraqi people as liberators from Hussein and their Sunni, Baathist oppressors. It all sounded so surrealistic that I sat in the meeting for the first ten minutes in utter disbelief at what I was hearing. Nothing so complex as overthrowing the regime of Hussein and the Baath Party and finding parity between Iraq's different ethnic and sectarian communities could be so easily explained as a military strategy lasting only three short days.

Discussing the cost of such an operation, the religious leaders were told that the total cost of this military engagement would only impact the United States Treasury by about $80 billion and most of that would be reimbursed by the sale of Iraqi oil.

I and several others asked about the intelligence the Pentagon said it had about Iraq possessing weapons of mass destruction. We were told that the evidence was clear and reliable: that Hussein possessed chemical and biological weapons and that since those weapons had been used by the Iraqi army against Iranian troops in the Iran-Iraq war, he would deploy them again if need be against his neighbors and US military forces. There were hints that Iraq had also been working on developing a nuclear capability that was unacceptable to the United States and American interests in the Middle East. As religious leaders, we were reminded once again by the secretary of defense that Hussein was a Sunni secularist, wrapped up in the repressive and murderous policies of the Baath Party. Sunnis were a distinct Muslim minority in Iraq, and the minority repressed Iraq's Shia Muslim majority through terrorism, political assassinations, and torture, using every possible means of coercion available to maintain control. Likewise, the Kurds in northern Iraq had suffered a similar fate under Hussein. The evidence against Hussein, Rumsfeld and Wolfowitz asserted, required immediate action by the United States.

Religious representatives asked other questions about whether there was a correlation between poverty, feelings of hopelessness, humiliation, and unemployment that could be a leading cause of an increase in the rise of terrorism in the Middle East. We also asked whether the Pentagon and the administration had thought about what would happen after shock and awe, when the tables were turned on the religious leadership in that country, and the Shiites who had been repressed by the minority Sunnis gained the freedom to exert their influence and power over their political and religious oppressors. Those questions went unanswered, except for the one on poverty, which, we were told, was a question for the churches to address.

To say that this meeting was painful and short-sighted and that shock and awe was a highly simplistic and poorly thought out military and foreign policy dictum is an understatement. I left the Pentagon that day crestfallen, convinced that unless mainline religious leaders and their denominations joined together in their support of the administration's plan to invade Iraq, our religious voices of opposition would be marginalized and our opposition to the war muted. Carter's words were now becoming true: "but the greater threat comes when the church is no longer kept merely separate but is forced into a position of utter subservience, its voice disregarded in the greater public discussions or even disqualified from joining them." For me on that day it was a forgone conclusion that the decision had already been made to invade Iraq. The only question was when such an invasion would take place.

We know now that churches were not the only institution in the United States to face withering pressure from the administration. Journalists in the print and electronic media were pressured to mute their criticism of emerging war plans and to get behind the president. Likewise, Congress had come under the spell of an administration clearly committed to engaging Iraq in a military campaign. Efforts by the religious community to encourage opposition to the use of force authorization in Congress were rebuffed. Congress's myopic compliance in granting the administration's wishes to go to war with, at best, paper-thin evidence that Iraq possessed weapons of mass destruction was shocking—even shameful. In its actions, Congress revealed a very painful and shallow understanding of the situation in Iraq or a craven political calculation, or both. In the end, it appeared politics prevailed over conscience.

In retrospect, it is clear that the United States and the American people were still in a state of shock from the terrorist attacks against the World Trade Center and the Pentagon. The administration was using a strategy of fear to push its agenda of preemptive warfare against Iraq. The administration pushed evidence later deemed fallacious that Iraq had purchased yellowcake for the purpose of manufacturing nuclear weapons, they had mobile chemical weapons labs, and they were in possession of major stockpiles of chemical and biological weapons that made Iraq one of the most dangerous countries in the Middle East. Information later revealed to be untrue linking al Qaeda with Iraq's military leaders, and Hussein was the final piece of the puzzle the administration used to convince the American people that war with Iraq was necessary and inevitable. The case for going to war with Iraq had been made to the American people and dissenting voices had all but been eliminated.

Leaders of the religious community opposing the war were now effectively marginalized by the administration, Congress, and the media. Our frustration as religious leaders mounted day by day, and in my case many of my parishioners in the diocese of Washington wondered out loud why the voices of the faith community opposing the war were not being heard, why our op-eds against the war were not being published, and why the media for the most part had shunned our collective voices of opposition.

Frustrated beyond measure, Jim Wallis of Sojourners and I decided to bring together the broad wings of the evangelical community and mainline Christian denominations in an effort to speak with a unified voice to make one last stand to force the administration to use the soft power of negotiation rather than the hard power of military action. Together we held a conference at the National Press Club in Washington on the merits of the just war theory, joined by religious voices from both the United States and Great Britain. Later, Jim and I were invited to present our case at a State Department program known as the Secretary's Open Forum where Kenneth Pollock was the keynote speaker that day. A former member of the Clinton administration, Pollock spoke eloquently that future military action might be an option, but that such action taken at this time was flawed. And in his opinion it would take at least fifty years to establish a form of Western-style democracy that was being pushed by the then-current administration. Following the forum, we were invited to attend a private and secured luncheon with staff members serving under Secretary of State Powell.

Our efforts as religious leaders were obviously failing and time was running out. The president refused to meet with us, but rather chose to meet with a handful of representatives from the religious right and with evangelist Billy Graham. Frustrated, we decided to take our case to Great Britain to meet with Prime Minister Blair, a meeting arranged by Claire Short, a member of Parliament, a close friend of Wallis's. We were joined by a broad coalition of religious leaders from the United States, representing mainline Christian denominations and evangelicals as well Anglican bishops from Great Britain, South Africa, Jerusalem, and the Middle East. For more than one hour we pleaded with Prime Minister Blair to exercise whatever influence he had as an ally of President Bush to rethink the implications of military action against Iraq. We were not successful in persuading the prime minister to alter what we now saw as inevitable military action, and we returned to the United States tired and discouraged. Carter's warning about the removal of faith from public life was no longer an academic prophecy but was now a painful reality.

As a last resort, Wallis and I decided to coauthor an op-ed that ran in *The Washington Post* on March 14, 2003, just a few short days before the United States invaded Iraq. Entitled "There Is a Third Way," the article raised our concerns about the consequences of a preemptive war with Iraq: high civilian and military casualties, setting a precedent for other preemptive wars, further destabilization of the Middle East, and the fueling of a massive wave of terrorism. Following publication of the article, we were contacted by many people both in- and outside of government who said that it was a solid piece of writing but came too late to affect the decision already made by the Bush administration to go to war.

Since that op-ed, and since we committed our military to invade Iraq, over four thousand brave American servicemen and servicewomen have lost their lives, well over thirty thousand have been wounded, many so severely that their lives as civilians will forever be altered. Iraqi casualties are hard to estimate, but numbers are conservatively calculated to exceed fifty thousand. A war that the Pentagon experts said would cost the American people $80 billion has now ballooned to a total estimated cost of over $1 trillion. The costs for ongoing medical care covering the wounded and disabled through the Department of Veterans Affairs medical facilities are horrendous and much of the expense has yet to be determined. Financially, the United States will be paying for this war many long years after it is over.

For the faith community, as we engage the challenges of the twenty-first century, war is the ultimate definition of human failure. As a nation we have failed from the outset in understanding the religious and cultural dimensions that define Iraq. Sunni divisions widen, Shia clerics call for the reestablishment of Sharia law, Sufis are a threatened minority, as are the Kurds in the north, and women in Iraq are worse off now than they were when Hussein ruled. As a government, the administration's understanding and knowledge of Islam was at best elementary.

It is this arrogance and ignorance coupled with Congress's foxholed political leadership in understanding the role of religion and faith and its negative and positive impact on the domestic and global scene that has contributed heavily to the current position in Iraq and the Middle East. Now we must call on moderates representing the dominant religious traditions that define the world's geopolitical scene to come together in a series of global summits to begin in earnest the kind of relational theological dialogue that has been, so far, loosely occurring throughout the world, but has not yet found any unifying forum from which to work. Religion and exercising one's faith in public life is not the cause of terrorism; neither is it to be blamed for the crisis in the Middle East, but nonetheless it is the fault line for these conflicts. The use of indiscriminant violence and military force, mindless terrorism, and religious hegemony must no longer be acceptable as a means to an end.

The global religious community in all of its configurations must now do what we have failed to do in the past: come together for the common good of all humanity, basing our actions on the compassion, radical hospitality, and search for universal peace that the holy books of the Abrahamic tradition have always called us to claim.

PART TWO
The Conduct of the War

Too Little, Too Late: Societal Transformation on a Shoestring Is No Strategy

Daniel Christman

America's Iraq venture is likely to be the most influential event shaping US diplomatic and military strategy for the first half of this century. Like other tectonic events of the twentieth century—the two world wars, Korea, the Cuban Missile Crisis, Vietnam—Iraq will inspire analysts to divine multiple meanings from our experience and draw conclusions that will impact, for better or worse, US international conduct through ensuing decades. Like these earlier events, Iraq will be analyzed through multiple prisms, shedding light on every element of national decision making and national power.

My focus, however, is on the achievement of strategic goals and the classic dilemma of aligning ends with means. David Ignatius, writing in the *The Washington Post*, captured the point when he simply stated: "Don't attempt a wholesale transformation of another society unless you have the troops and political will to impose it."

Few Iraq issues have been more openly debated than the sufficiency of army and marine force structure for Operation Iraqi Freedom (OIF). The bottom line, however, is increasingly clear: national decision makers, including senior military commanders, negligently failed to plan for adequate force levels, particularly for the so-called Phase IV of OIF—the postcombat phase that would stabilize and rebuild a fractured Iraqi society and economy.

What Phase IV planning was done was performed late, with little interagency coordination and with pathetically few troops to execute what, by any reasonable assessment, was a monumental undertaking. The lack of sufficient ground forces precluded adequate border security, the seizure and destruction of Hussein's munitions stockpiles, and the defeat of countless insurgent groups that mushroomed in the waning days of the active combat phase.

The unwillingness of Secretary Rumsfeld and President Bush to consider adjustments to the overall force structure in Iraq earlier than 2007 looms as one of the most significant mistakes—and lessons learned—of the entire Iraq tragedy. As Ignatius cautioned, we faced nothing less than the wholesale transformation of an ancient society, and it was intellectual hubris to think we could accomplish this task with the forces allocated.

But wholesale transformations take more than troops; they also take time. And the time given to forces of a democracy bent on societal change abroad is a direct function of the ability of national command authorities to marshal political will. In this dimension as well—the building of political consensus and public support that are essential underpinnings of will in a democracy—the administration that took us to war in Iraq left behind a sad trail of vital lessons.

Americans are quintessentially a five-minute culture. Marshaling and sustaining public support for any national undertaking is a Herculean task, made even more challenging by a twenty-four-hour news cycle that demands clarity of purpose and consistent, credible articulation of strategy and long-term goals. If properly informed about issues, Americans will follow leaders who ask for their support. Our successes in the cold war, in space, and in desegregation, stand out as twentieth-century examples of successes made possible by building and sustaining domestic political will.

Engaging in a long-term struggle against an extremist ideology will be the most significant challenge for our country in the decades ahead. Simply stated, we must be far more adept as a nation in reaching out to the media and using information in ways that build national consensus and international legitimacy. Iraq has hardly been the model for future national leaders bent on building the will for a vital international undertaking. Indeed, OIF illustrates tragically how will can evaporate if national leaders view such ventures through narrow, unilateral, partisan, and ideological filters.

National security planners have always faced a resource challenge in drafting workable constructs for overseas operations. Regardless of perceived national priorities, there are rarely sufficient resources to satisfy on-scene commanders. For this reason, the most fundamental rule that guides planners is to align troops to task and to follow national strategic guidance in overall force allocations.

Listen to advice from a broad array of military and

civilian experts to decide on troop numbers, be flexible in adjusting plans after the first shot is fired, and build the necessary political will to sustain the operation are all axioms learned early on by even the most junior force planner. Collectively they constitute the most significant lesson *relearned* from our undertaking in Iraq.

Iraq War Planners
Ignored Powerful Historic Lessons

Robert D. Hormats

A central lesson that should be learned from the war in Iraq is that a successful outcome requires both over-whelming force and a compelling political strategy that forges strong international and in-country alliances. The two must go together.

In the first military exercise this nation undertook—putting down the Whiskey Rebellion in western Pennsylvania in 1794—Alexander Hamilton advised President George Washington that, although there were few insurgents, the federal government should send a massive force of thirteen thousand men. He argued that "Whenever the government appears in arms, it ought to appear like Hercules." This Hamilton Doctrine, which preceded the Powell Doctrine by two centuries, was invoked by Washington at the time, and the insurrection melted away. Neither President Bush nor Secretary Rumsfeld invoked the Powell Doctrine, and we have seen the consequences.

In Iraq, the United States also failed on a second count—to implement a comprehensive political strategy. The coalition was a pale version of the one assembled to fight the first Iraq war: no Middle Eastern or Muslim nations, few European nations, and no financial support from anyone else. And our leaders failed to forge an effective political strategy to shore up support among key communities in Iraq. A meaningful outreach strategy in Iraq backed by considerably greater numbers of troops to protect Iraqis and their economic infrastructure could have improved chances for success and held down the number of American and Iraqi casualties.

Generals George C. Marshall and Dwight D. Eisenhower recognized during World War II that winning a modern war depends not only on massive force, but also on the application of considerable political and diplomatic skills—building and holding together a strong international coalition and working closely with in-country groups after the war to establish a solid and durable peace. These profound understandings were crucial to success in the greatest war in American history. Planning for the Iraq war ignored these powerful historic lessons.

Less bravado, better planning, more troops, an effective alliance, and a sounder strategy for garnering domestic allies in Iraq to forge a stable peace would have significantly improved US prospects.

Reaping an Uncertain Result: American Media and the Iraq War

Steven Livingston

In 2003, when the United States was at the cusp of an elective conflict with Iraq, the press's democratic accountability function was encumbered by professional norms that made it unwilling, if not unable, to challenge the predicates of war offered by American political leaders. Then, while in the midst of the conflict, the press lost sight of bigger questions and instead allowed itself to become embroiled in controversies about taste and propriety. Finally, as the war in Iraq bled on into a more-than-six-year slog, the press simply lost interest and went home. In short, we can now see that the press failed in its obligation to hold authorities accountable for the war and its aftermath. This is the lesson of Iraq and the American press.

Criticism of news coverage of the Iraq war reached a zenith early on, focusing on the press's failure to challenge the Bush administration's preinvasion claims about weapons of mass destruction and al Qaeda connections to Saddam Hussein's Baathist regime in Baghdad.[1] In more recent years, criticism has tended to focus on questions of propriety and taste in how specific events have been reported.[2] In 2008, for example, a suicide bomber killed three marines, two interpreters, and several Iraqi civilians. Freelance photojournalist Zoriah Miller was embedded with the nearby marine unit that responded to the blast. His photographs captured a terrible scene of carnage, including several pictures of the dead marines. In reporting the event, *The New York Times* ran a photograph of a body draped in a white sheet, someone killed in a separate blast elsewhere; the *Washington Post* story about the incident ran without photographs.[3] Miller, however, posted his images to his website after waiting for the marines to notify families.[4] As a result of his actions, he was barred from marine units in Anbar province.[5] Some believed the marines and the press sanitized the event, while others thought Miller showed poor taste in photographing the dead marines and posting the pictures to his website. Except for occasional event-specific controversies like this, though, criticism of the press in Iraq has been surprisingly muted. Similar criticism, it's worth noting, was largely lacking when it came to widespread reproduction of the gruesome images of the bodies of Abu Musab al-Zarqawi and Uday and Qusay Hussein, all enemies of the United States.

Part of the explanation for the silence is found in the general recognition that journalists, whether American or Iraqi, have faced enormous and often deadly challenges in covering the war. As of February 2009, 223 journalists and media assistants have been killed in Iraq. Nowhere have so many journalist been killed trying to report a story. What have we reaped for the toll paid by so many journalists?

On the whole, American media coverage of Iraq has shown occasional flashes of brilliance. For instance, *The Washington Post*'s Steve Fainaru's Pulitzer Prize–winning investigation of a private security contractor's apparent trigger-happy practices was superb.[6] Anthony Shadid, also of the *Post*, won a Pulitzer in 2004 for his insightful and fearless war reporting from Iraq. On these shores, CBS's *60 Minutes* and Seymour Hersh of *The New Yorker* led the way in reporting the Abu Ghraib prison abuse and torture story. There are of course many other exemplar moments of individual reporting. But on the whole, and at a more *systematic* level, American news organizations long ago abandoned Iraq. In doing so, they failed to offer a full and complete picture of a war that will, before it is over, burn through trillions of dollars, destroy tens of thousands of lives, and quite possibly reorder the balance of power in the Middle East.

If from 2008 through 2009 the American people and political leadership debated the merits of an accelerated military withdrawal from Iraq, American news organizations had long before conducted their own unilateral withdrawal. It began in September 2007 when General Petraeus testified before Congress and reported that the surge, the US–troop reinforcement, had been accompanied by a marked decline in sectarian violence. With that, President Bush declared the surge a success, with the press following suit. In doing so, the press showed itself incapable of learning from prior mistakes, the very ones the *Times* and *Post* apologized for committing in 2002 through 2003: credulously accepting the White House's framing of the Iraq story.[7]

That was the turning point. In the nine months following General Petraeus's testimony, the three broadcast networks' nightly newscasts *combined* devoted an average of six minutes a week to Iraq. In contrast to the entire previous five-year period, the networks each averaged twenty-six minutes per week.[8] After 2007, CBS News no longer stationed a full-time correspondent in Iraq, a circumstance that led CBS war correspondent Lara Logan to declare on Jon Stewart's *The Daily Show*, "If I were to watch the news that you hear here in the United States, I would just blow my brains out because it would drive me nuts."[9]

Similarly, the Pew Research Center's Project for Excellence in Journalism found that just 4 percent of total news space allocation was devoted to the Iraq war from January 1 to March 20, 2008. Iraq was yesterday's news to American media. The graph on page 41 of 2008 news coverage of Iraq created by the Project for Excellence in Journalism illustrates the press's fading interest in Iraq.[10]

This precipitous decline in media attention began taking a toll on public awareness of even the most basic and compelling facts about the war, such as the total number of US casualties. By March 2008, just 28 percent of adults in the United States were able to say that approximately four thousand Americans had been killed while serving in Iraq.[11]

As tragic as is the death of so many US soldiers and marines, the greater catastrophe might well be found in the geopolitical costs of the war. To appreciate this point requires us to think back to 2002 and 2003 and remember what was proposed as a possible geopolitical consequence of the war.

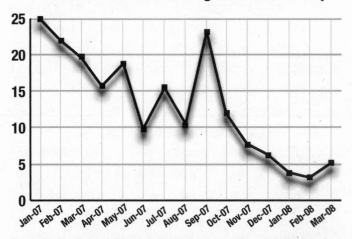

Percent of News Coverage Devoted to Iraq

Source: The Pew Research Center's Project for Excellence in Journalism, "Iraq War Coverage Plunges," March 25, 2008. The data is accessible at www.journalism.org/node/10345.

A liberated Iraq, it was suggested before the war, would serve as a democratic role model for the rest of the Arab world. This represented a mainstream media consensus ranging from the liberal *New York Times* columnist Thomas L. Friedman to the neoconservative Charles Krauthammer, both enthusiastic proponents of this rationale. An unstated purpose of the war, Friedman averred, was to "transform it [Iraq] from a totalitarian system that has threatened its neighbors and its own people into something better." Post-Hussein Iraq would serve, he said, "as a progressive model to spur reform—educational, religious, economic and political—around the Arab world."[12] Similarly, Krauthammer, writing in *The Washington Post* in February 2002, drew a line that led from a liberated Iraq to regime change in Iran. "Overthrowing neighboring radical regimes [Iraq] shows the fragility of dictatorship, challenges the mullahs' mandate from heaven and thus encourages disaffected Iranians to rise." The effort would begin, said Krauthammer, with "Afghanistan to the east. Next, Iraq to the west." Theocratic Iran would then collapse. It hasn't worked out that way.

While the press helped propagate the notion of a post-Hussein Iraq as a democratic beacon in the region, it has failed to draw attention to the actual geopolitical consequences of the war after they became apparent. *This is the central failing of the press concerning the Iraq war.* Former ambassador Peter Galbraith made the point succinctly: "Insurgency, civil war, Iranian strategic triumph, the breakup of Iraq, an independent Kurdistan, military quagmire. These are all consequences of the American invasion of Iraq that the Bush administration failed to anticipate."[13] The press failed to report this counternarrative in any systematic way, instead continuing to rely heavily on the Bush administration's upbeat assessments of every potential nugget of good news mined from the deep quarry of bad news.

Of all the unintended consequences of the Iraq war, Iran's strategic ascendance is perhaps the most consequential. To put it in perspective, the Treaty of Qasr-e Shirin in 1639 established the border between the Persian Shia and Ottoman Sunni empires after more than a century of conflict. Three centuries later, an eight-year war between Iran and Iraq took one million lives but failed to fundamentally alter the divide. That changed in 2003 with the American invasion of Iraq. "The US invasion of Iraq in 2003," noted Galbraith, accomplished what Khomeini's army could not. Today, the Shiite-controlled lands extend to the borders of Kuwait and Saudi Arabia...[and] Bahrain."[14]

This was a potential history-changing realignment of the Middle East. Yet, as far as the American press is concerned, it might all just as well be the history of Mars. The hope of conveying meaningful and sophisticated coverage about Iraq and regional geopolitics has all but evaporated.

For example, in the aftermath of the 2009 Iraqi provincial assembly elections—elections that were the best barometer of the political consequences of the troop surge—readers were treated to coverage that looked more like coverage of the New Hampshire primaries, though on the Tigris. *The New York Times* used a conventional horse-race election press formula of "who's ahead and who's behind" in its analysis of the election results. Prime Minister Nouri al-Maliki's Dawa Party was in the lead!

In short, the American press has given up what little fight it had in it to dig deeper into Iraqi politics and to develop a picture of the geopolitical effects of a misbegotten war. As a result, the American people are left unsure of the sacrifice of more than four thousand servicemen and servicewomen who have died—and the trillion dollars invested—for what is at best an ambiguous political outcome. The press has left us unaware of both the depth of the sacrifice paid by so many and the consequence we all shall reap in years to come.

Notes

1. W. Lance Bennett, Regina G. Lawrence, and Steven Livingston, *When the Press Fails: Political Power and the News Media from Iraq to Katrina* (Chicago: Univ. of Chicago Press, 2007); Steven Kull, "Misperceptions, the Media and the Iraq War," The PIPA/ Knowledge Network Poll, October 2, 2003, www.worldpublic opinion.org/pipa/pdf/oct03/IraqMedia_Oct03_rpt.pdf. Both *The Washington Post* and *The New York Times* published critical assessments of their own coverage during the lead-up to the war. For an apology offered by *The New York Times* for its failures in the Iraq war, see "The Times and Iraq," May 26, 2004; for *The Washington Post*, see Howard Kurtz, "The Post on WMDs: The Inside Story," *The Washington Post*, Aug. 12, 2004, A01.

2. Kevin Sites, "What happened in the Fallujah mosque: NBC correspondent writes about the killing of an injured Iraqi," MSNBC .com, May 4, 2005, www.msnbc.msn.com/id/6556034/.

3. Allisa J. Rubin, "3 US Marines and More than 30 Iraqis Die in 2 Bomb Attacks," *The New York Times*, June 27, 2008. www.nytimes .com/2008/06/27/world/middleeast/27iraq.html?ex=137230560 0&en=007fb720eb986274&ei=5124&partner=permalink&expr

od=permalink; Ernesto Londono, "Marines, Interpreters Among Those Killed in Iraq Attacks," *The Washington Post*, June 26, 2008, www.washingtonpost.com/wp-dyn/content/article/2008/06/26/AR2008062602412.html?hpid=moreheadlines.

4. Zoriah Photojournalist, "Suicide Bombing in Anbar," www.zoriah.net/blog/suicide-bombing-in-anbar-.html.

5. The *Times* eventually published one of Miller's photographs. It accompanied a story about the paucity of images of dead soldiers and marines after so many years of fighting and so many deaths. See Michael Kamber and Tim Arango, "4,000 US Deaths, and a Handful of Images," *The New York Times*, July 26, 2008.

6. Steve Fainaru, "Guards in Iraq Cite Frequent Shootings Companies Seldom Report Incidents, US Officials Say," *The Washington Post*, Oct. 3, 2007, A01.

7. See Robert Entman, Steven Livingston, and Jennie Kim, "Doomed to Repeat: Iraq News 2002–2007," *American Behavioral Scientist* 51 (January 2009).

8. Tyndall Report, "2008 Year in Review," http://tyndallreport.com/yearinreview2008/.

9. The Huffington Post, June 18, 2008, www.huffingtonpost.com/2008/06/18/cbss-lara-logan-slams-ame_n_107914.html.

10. Pew Research Center for the People & the Press, "Awareness of Iraq War Fatalities Plummets," http://people-press.org/report/401/.

11. Pew Research Center, http://people-press.org/report/401/.

12. Thomas L. Friedman, "Will the Neighbors Approve?," *The New York Times*, February 5, 2003.

13. Peter W. Galbraith, *The End of Iraq* (New York: Simon & Schuster, 2006), 7.

14. Peter W. Galbraith, *Unintended Consequences: How the War in Iraq Strengthened America's Enemies* (New York: Simon & Schuster, 2008), 28.

A Responsibility to Learn

John A. Nagl

During a long, hard fight in Vietnam, the United States Army learned a great deal about how to wage counterinsurgency effectively, particularly under the leadership of General Creighton Abrams. Unfortunately, much of that learning came after Americans had grown tired of the war in Vietnam, and the lessons did not take root; in fact, they were actively expunged from the army's institutional memory in the wake of a deeply unpopular war. We are now fighting another great counterinsurgency campaign. After a slow start, we have relearned the lessons that were purchased so dearly in Vietnam. We owe it to those who have fallen in this fight, both American and Iraqi, to vow that we will never again purge ourselves of the knowledge and ability to fight insurgents effectively.

Rather than rethinking and improving its counterinsurgency doctrine after Vietnam, the army sought to bury it, largely banishing it from its key field manuals and the curriculum of its schoolhouses. The army's superlative performance in Operation Desert Storm in 1991 further entrenched the mind-set that conventional state-on-state warfare was the future, while counterinsurgency and irregular warfare were but lesser included contingencies.

The army did not adjust to the fact that its peer competitor had collapsed, spending the decade after the end of the cold war continuing to prepare for war against a Soviet Union that no longer existed. Deployments to Somalia, Haiti, and the Balkans in the 1990s brought the army face to face with different types of missions that did not adhere to the Desert Storm model, but despite the relatively high demand for its forces in unconventional environments, the army continued to emphasize rapid, decisive battlefield operations by large combat forces in its doctrine and professional education. The overriding emphasis on conventional operations left the army unable to deal effectively with the war in Iraq.

The army's lack of preparedness for counterinsurgency in Iraq was exacerbated by its failure to adapt fully and rapidly to its demands. The fall of Baghdad in April 2003 after a three-week campaign initially appeared as another confirmation of the superiority of US military capabilities, but the enemy had other plans. Inadequate contingency planning by both civilian leaders and military commanders to secure the peace contributed to the chaotic conditions that enabled insurgent groups to establish themselves. With some notable lower-level exceptions, the institutional army did not adapt to these conditions until it was perilously close to losing this war.

US forces faced with insurgencies had no doctrinal or training background in irregular warfare and reacted in an ad hoc fashion to challenges. Many early approaches to counterinsurgency failed to protect the population from insurgent attacks and alienated the people through the excessive use of force. Although some units did develop and employ effective population-centric counterinsurgency techniques independently, such improvements were not emulated in a coordinated fashion throughout the force. It was not until 2007 that the army finally adopted a unified approach that effectively secured the population and co-opted reconcilable insurgent fighters in Iraq..

The brave efforts and sacrifices of American soldiers have added up to less than the sum of their parts due to institutional resistance to change. Even as counterinsurgency learning percolated throughout the ranks, the Department of Defense was slow to recognize the need to adapt its doctrine, organization, training, and procurement priorities to ensure that its forces were properly prepared for the wars they were fighting. The failure to quickly provide sufficient quantities of up-armored Humvees, Mine Resistant Ambush Protected vehicles, and surveillance equipment to troops in the field is illustrative of an organization practicing business as usual at a time of crisis.

Lack of urgency amid rapidly changing circumstances is a theme that has run throughout the army's handling of Iraq. The army clung to the failing strategy of rapidly transitioning security responsibility to indigenous forces as Iraq fell into chaos in 2006 and persistently resisted calls for troop increases to provide population security. The critical mission of training and advising allied security forces has been severely underresourced and is still organized and manned in makeshift fashion, despite the fact that victory in this struggle depends on America's ability to develop capable host-nation security forces.

In many ways, the army has still not institutionalized the lessons of six years of fighting in Iraq. Battalion commanders leading counterinsurgency operations as part of the surge in 2007 and 2008 still had not read noted theorist David Galula, or the other essential texts on counterinsurgency. Useful tools to secure and control the population, such as biometric identification measures, are still in short supply. No institutional doctrine guides the still–ad hoc effort to advise the Iraqi security forces. And there is still no systematic attempt to inculcate the hard-won truths about the wars of today into the next generation of soldiers.

A close look at the historical record reveals that the United States engages in ambiguous counterinsurgency and nation-building missions far more often than it faces full-scale war. Just since the end of the cold war, American troops have been deployed to make and keep the peace in such strategic backwaters as Somalia, Bosnia, and Kosovo. Similar demands will only increase in a globalized world where local problems increasingly do not stay local and where trends such as the youth bulge and urbanization in underdeveloped states, as well as the proliferation of more lethal weaponry, point to a future dominated by chaotic local insecurity and conflict rather than confrontations between the armies and navies of nation-states. The US military is more likely to be called upon to counter insurgencies, intervene in civil strife and humanitarian crises, rebuild nations, and wage unconventional types of warfare than it is to fight mirror-image armed forces. It will not have the luxury of opting out of these missions because they do not conform to preferred notions of the American way of war.

The developing strategic environment will find state

and non-state adversaries devising innovative strategies to counter American military power by exploiting widely available technology and weapons and integrating tactics from across the spectrum of conflict. The resulting conflicts will be protracted and hinge on the affected populations' perceptions of truth and legitimacy rather than the outcome of tactical engagements on the battlefield. Interestingly, they sound similar to the insurgencies that the United States is currently combating, only more difficult. The learning curve is not going to get any easier.

The US Army has adapted to the demands of counterinsurgency over the past few years—but too painfully, fitfully, and slowly. As Secretary of Defense Gates has noted, "In Iraq, we've seen how an army that was basically a smaller version of the cold war force can over time become an effective instrument of counterinsurgency. But that came at a frightful human, financial, and political cost." While individual soldiers and units have much to be proud of, the institutional army's record of counterinsurgency adaptation to the current conflicts leaves much to be desired. Thousands of lives were lost while soldiers and their leaders struggled to learn how to deal with an unfamiliar situation. At least some of those losses might have been avoided had the army and defense community at large learned from rather than discounted past lessons and experiences.

The US military's role in irregular warfare cannot be wished or willed away, and the army has a responsibility to prepare itself to fulfill that role as effectively as possible. We who have learned these lessons at such great cost must ensure that they are never again forgotten.

Rediscovering the Real Lessons of Vietnam

Bernard I. Finel

As the Iraq war dragged on, a consensus emerged that a major problem was the United States had forgotten the lessons of Vietnam. Within the army in particular, several senior leaders, notably General Petraeus, sought to popularize and institutionalize counterinsurgency doctrine as a means to better fight the war in Iraq. Unfortunately, the key lesson of Vietnam was not the methods of fighting insurgencies, but rather the folly of engaging in such wars under most circumstances.

Prior generations also wrestled with lessons of Vietnam. Indeed, the army in the 1970s did not seek to forget Vietnam as much as it sought to ensure that the United States never again tried to wage a long, grinding counterinsurgency without asking for full commitment and sacrifice from the American public. When General Creighton Abrams transformed army personnel policies to ensure that the reserves would have to be mobilized for any major combat operation, he sought to ensure that commitments like Vietnam were broadly supported by the American public, and as a result rare.

In a profound sense, the current generation of lessons of Vietnam are wholly at odds with the lessons actually learned by the men who fought and led during that conflict. Instead of trying to avoid such engagements, the current counterinsurgency theorists seem keen to establish a force that will find it easier and more likely to fight these kinds of war. The problem is the doctrine is wrong and the goal is largely unachievable.

Defeating an insurgency through foreign intervention is a once-in-a-blue-moon achievement. The very structure of the conflict places the counterinsurgency forces at a massive disadvantage. First, counterinsurgents need to provide services, security, and legitimacy. Insurgents merely need to prevent that from occurring. It is easier to burn a school than to build one. A single bomb creates insecurity, even if nine others were successfully defused. Second, any external intervention begins with a presumption of illegitimacy. Foreign troops almost always look like an occupation rather than a liberation, especially when the differences are heightened by cultural, linguistic, and religious divides. Armed English-speaking Christians of European and African descent are never going to be particularly welcome in the Muslim world, for instance. Third, insurgents win by simply not losing. Their strength comes from persistence, which is precisely what foreign interveners from democratic states lack.

Preparing to fight counterinsurgencies is a strategically incoherent approach that ensures that the United States will engage in combat under the worst possible conditions. We are like a passing team in football that chooses, deliberately, to play in the snow and wind.

A major problem we face in avoiding the strategic

blunder of building a counterinsurgency force is the current status of civil-military relations in the United States. We have built a closed, self-reinforcing loop that marginalizes strategic assessment in the decision-making process. Having been asked to fight a counterinsurgency, military leaders are quite reasonably concerned that they will be asked to do so again. Purely as a matter of training and equipping the force, military leaders have begun to press to make the military more focused on these kinds of missions. Seeing that military leaders are moving toward building a counterinsurgency force, political leaders, in the name of supporting the troops, are lining up behind these transformations. In this way, reluctant steps by the military to hedge against future requirements become justifications for enshrining those requirements as the essence of national strategy.

Military leaders are imbued with a can-do spirit that leads them to make the best of bad situations, to try to do more with less, and generally to focus on problem solving. But unfortunately, this attitude removes what could be the most persuasive voices for reconsideration from the public debate. When faced with the prospect of a proliferation of Iraq-like conflicts, military leaders ought to be saying, "Hell no," or at least, "Are you sure you want to do this?" Instead, what they are saying is "We'll be asked to do this sort of thing anyway, so we might as well prepare for it."

There is, in truth, a fine line between respectful advocacy of controversial opinions and the prospect of insubordination. But there is also a fine line between responsiveness to civilian leadership and the mute acceptance of strategically disastrous military policies. At this point, the uniformed military needs to rediscover its post-Vietnam antipathy to nation-building and counterinsurgency and make a principled case to avoid, or at least dramatically limit, the cases in which it is called upon to operate in these environments.

The lesson of Iraq should be that conflicts of this sort are longer, costlier, and much more difficult than anticipated. And instead of thinking about how to fight them better in the future, we should be concentrating our energies on avoiding such contingencies when possible. The war in Iraq was, unquestionably, a war of choice. Let's not allow a bad decision there to tempt us into repeating the folly in the hopes of doing better next time.

How We Leave Matters

Lee F. Gunn

I hate this war and believe we should not have invaded Iraq. But this war, and the way we end it, will have profound implications for America's future use of force and our exercise of political will in the world. When we leave Iraq, we must do so in a way that protects American military power and manages others' perceptions of that power in order to avoid unintended—and potentially bloody—consequences in the future.

Instead of seeking to draw lessons from the Iraq experience that we may apply to future conflicts, my goal is to consider how we can apply what we already know to the current situation in Iraq in order to ensure that we draw this conflict to a close in a way that does not further endanger US security.

There are four critical points to consider. First, America's military is the strongest, most flexible, hardest hitting, and most compassionate the world has ever known. Second, until Operation Iraqi Freedom, the excellence of America's military was almost universally acknowledged and its capabilities feared. Third, this respect remains, but our enemies have exposed some vulnerabilities to tactics for which we should have prepared.

And fourth, this respect (and fear) must be preserved as we wind down our involvement in the war.

Our extraordinary military will be asked again to protect American security and enable the other elements of our national power. Accordingly, the manner in which we leave Iraq is as important now as how we invaded. We must emerge from Iraq with armed forces that continue to be seen around the world as "your best friend and your worst enemy."

We must learn from our experiences, and our experience in Iraq is not new. We fought and mismanaged a similar war within the lifetime of the people who decided to wage this one. It seems that we learned little along the way.

In the midst of the cold war, we engaged in combat in Vietnam that showed, individual courage and determination aside, that the vaunted US military and its political masters could be fought to a standstill under certain circumstances. I believe that many of us who served in the armed forces then feared, during the decadelong rebuilding of our military, that we would be tested again and found to be wanting.

Notwithstanding the above, it's safe to say that the US military emerged from the cold war with a reputation for unmatched competence, admirable restraint, and crushing capability. As if to demonstrate that the reputation was deserved, the United States succeeded both politically and militarily in the 1990s: preparing for the first Gulf War, then winning in the desert, prodding Europe into belated action, and then leading the way in the Balkans. Later still, the United States saved hundreds of thousands of lives in East Africa where we and our allies—despite later portrayals to the contrary—accomplished a daunting humanitarian mission in Somalia. In all that busy time, the men and women of our armed forces added in many ways to their aura of invincibility.

American and coalition forces quickly seized the planned initial military objectives in the Iraq war. Shortly afterward, things changed in unexpected and unplanned ways. Since then, the war in Iraq has exposed our forces to surprising threats and a degree of instability that neither our defense investments in equipment nor training had prepared them to face.

As in Vietnam, enemies have shown that US forces are vulnerable to low-tech, irregular warfare. Insurgents and Iraqi terrorists have shown that there are at least temporary limits to America's military power. In a sense, we ceded to them the ability to define for the world our military capabilities and limitations.

Candid answers to important questions might help us avoid this situation in the future, assuming we are prepared to win on the battlefield. Are we ready to manage the aftermath? Can we understand and shape the post-event consequences? Will we learn and adapt to meet subsequent risks? Ultimately, will we emerge a stronger nation, militarily and politically? We must assess military engagements—and disengagements—in terms of their long-term impact on American power and influence, as well as immediate security objectives.

"Finishing what we've started in Iraq." What does that mean?

Our war in Iraq, and the way we end it, will have profound implications in setting the stage for future American political and military influence and operations. Discussions today of the way forward in Iraq fall mostly into two classes. In the first, it is argued that US and dwindling coalition forces must put in place conditions that permit the Iraqi Army and Police, under the central government, to assume responsibility for security. Only when this state is achieved can we leave Iraq. In the second class, observers argue that the American investment in lives and dollars is as great as it should have ever been and that the military should begin to withdraw now. In both cases it is generally accepted that an orderly withdrawal from Iraq will require at least twelve to fourteen months once it has begun.

The critical question then is this: How will America's image and leadership position fare because of our actions on Iraq in the coming months and years? Of course we hope to be able to choose, with the Iraqis, the resolution that's good for them. But nearly as important is that our actions position us beyond Iraq most favorably to pick our future fights, select our battlegrounds, and choose the timing and pace of combat in the battles to come.

I propose a new look at the possible gains and losses of these next couple of years as we make choices and choose direction in the Iraq war. We should begin by following these two simple suggestions. First, avoid spending more precious time on simplistic allegations about culpability in the decision to invade Iraq. We have more important things to do. Second, change the tenor of the discussions about withdrawal. Focus on what's important: achieving an acceptable level of stability quickly, removing Iraq as a future battlefield for us insofar as possible, and emerging from this war with America's image as a restrained but impossibly overwhelming foe improved.

There is no magic in these ideas. The solution lies in America's leaders working together among themselves and with others. The reality is that there must be a political accommodation at home as well as in Iraq. Overseas, Iraq's neighbors, as well as our friends and allies, have serious stakes in salvaging this tough situation. They must be involved. To involve them, we must talk with them.

If we need more talented American leaders working on this than those who have the responsibility today, we should be able to come up with them. America is the world's strongest and most powerful nation and we require leaders who measure up to our principles and work to advance the country's interests. That's what elections are for.

We must have a strong, capable, agile, well-trained, and equipped military. It has to be prepared for all the relevant fights: against terrorists, drug cartels, pirates, nuclear proliferators, and against other nations when our national security demands. The military must be multilingual, culturally attuned, disciplined, temperate, restrained, and ferocious at the appropriate times.

Our military today is as fearsome an instrument of national power as has ever existed. When necessary in the future, it should specifically be feared, so leaving Iraq without considering the future military power and image of the United States would be a serious mistake. Iraqi and foreign insurgents must not be allowed to define the limits of American power for years to come.

The Lessons the World Has Learned

Thomas P. M. Barnett

Looking at the United States from the outside in, these are the primary lessons I think the world takes away from America's global war on terrorism under Bush-Cheney.

If I were a potential state-based adversary of the United States, I would take little comfort from America's record in Afghanistan and Iraq to date, primarily because its military has shown itself capable of learning how to better shape outcomes on the lower end of the conflict spectrum—its Achilles' heel since World War II. Worse, that capacity for learning has kept its casualty levels low enough to call into question the long-held assumption that, after Vietnam, America has the patience only for short wars.

Prior to Iraq and the painful evolution it forced upon the US military, the Powell Doctrine's focus on "overwhelming force" translated into a first-half team (war) with little to no capacity to go the distance (post-war). Thus, America's military power faced no strategic or kinetic limits, but suffered distinct process limits that invited asymmetrical responses.

Now, the key limit on America's use of force is operational capacity, meaning it's becoming a truly full-service cop, albeit one burdened by an impossibly large beat. As such, what America has relearned in Iraq concerning the utility of subcontracting security responsibility to incentivized locals (e.g., the Sunni awakening) will inevitably be applied on an international scale.

None of these realities bodes well for non-state enemies of globalization's advance, for they suggest that the United States—unlike Europe or Japan—is able to once again tap into its historical experience as a powerful integrator of economic frontiers. Although September 11 temporarily triggered America's profound rage, the long, hard postwar slogs in Iraq and Afghanistan have not sent America over any ideological cliff—as evidenced by Barack Obama's victory over John McCain.

As a result, adversarial non-state actors should recalculate assumptions about the desirability of attracting America's entry into perceived quagmires. Socializing your fight internationally doesn't elicit the binary benefits of the cold war, and if the Americans cannot be bled to exhaustion in any one conflict and will simply refuse to participate in additional ones once their perceived operational bandwidth is tapped, luring them into "imperial overreach" is unlikely to yield victory within an acceptable time frame.

While America plays Leviathan-like bodyguard to globalization's advance, its private sector is not the primary agent of integration today. In developing areas, that role falls increasingly and overwhelmingly to rising great powers such as India and China, whose militaries are nowhere near advanced to the point where they can defend their nation's far-flung global economic interests.

In both Beijing and New Delhi, those strategic awakenings are proceeding apace, creating new alliance opportunities for the United States.

Thus, identifying your state or movement as constituting some new wing of an anti-American coalition presents no significant advantages (beyond local recruitment efforts), because rising great powers aren't particularly interested in bankrolling such activity unless clear economic gains are in sight—and if they are, then there's no good reason to incur America's wrath in the bargain. Such great powers want to piggyback on America's Leviathan services where they can, picking up only the cheapest wins where they cannot.

If you're a significant state actor, it's smarter to do what the Russians did in Georgia: punch hard and fast and get your business done quickly so that it can be presented to Washington as a fait accompli in the manner of a police action. If the Americans are sufficiently tied down elsewhere, your chances to achieve your desired outcome are high, assuming you can tolerate the subsequent economic punishments imposed by those competing great powers angered by your deeds.

If you're a great power willing to go down this route, it's smart to imitate America's approach: define the alleged bad guys in ideologically appropriate terms, observe the implied rules of a UN-sanctioned operation, and immediately offer to internationalize the "peaceful resolution" once your objectives have been secured. Above all, present your intervention as a boon to global economic stability. Nothing kills America's sense of urgency better than a sense of avoiding unwanted responsibility.

If you're a small state subject to a great power's perceived sphere of influence, these are humbling days. Sobered by recent experiences, America's military leadership now possesses a crystal ball on low-intensity conflict akin to the one it's long had on the subject of nuclear escalation, meaning there will be no stumblin' bumblin' dashes to inadvertent great-power war à la 1914.

Finally, whether I'm a state-based or non-state actor, I would take one additional lesson: America remains a society that glorifies violence and has little trouble expressing itself in this manner internationally. America's relative ease in continuing to attract young recruits into its military—particularly its ground forces—is simply astonishing, as is the continuing irrelevance of its antiwar movement.

PART THREE

The War and Instruments of National Power (Nondefense)

The New Face of War

Arthur S. Obermayer

The conflict in Iraq is the new face of war. The last protracted US war where there were clearly marked battle lines with uniformed soldiers separating the two sides was the Korean War, over a half century ago. Since then, it has been difficult to distinguish friend from foe, and victory has become more elusive. Today, the United States has the most sophisticated and strongest military might in the world, but that alone is not enough to prevail. The conflict in Iraq is only the most recent example of this trend, and it provides important lessons for American policymakers and the public to consider.

Conflict today is asymmetric, encompassing terrorism, insurgency, and guerilla activities as the most effective reaction to an army that is overpowering on the battlefield. Individuals with limited resources can wreak havoc in almost any place of their choosing. They don't usually represent a country and can live anywhere while easily communicating with each other by mobile phone and the Internet. The enemy works and lives in the same places as innocent people. Even our smart bombs are not smart enough to target them based on their state of mind. Instead, we end up destroying property and infrastructure and killing many innocent civilians. Until we reassess what we have accomplished on the battlefield and learn that twenty-first-century warfare has a different goal, all of our victories will be illusions.

Americans are disturbed and frustrated with the tactics used by the enemy, who are wiser than we are prepared to admit. Our adversaries seek to protect themselves, but also to win the hearts and minds of people. Collective punishment for the acts of a few creates fear and hatred among the impacted communities. When their way of life is destroyed and friends and family killed, they view the remote and callous Americans as causing wanton devastation. When the horrors of it are immediately seen on the TV screen, new enemies are created, not only in the country attacked, but also in the rest of the world. This is especially true among those people who feel cultural or religious bonds with those attacked.

Recent history has repeatedly demonstrated this failure. One of Osama bin Laden's goals was to encourage a military response from us that would generate more support for al Qaeda, and he succeeded. Initially, Hamas and Hezbollah gained strength by providing impoverished Arab villages free essential social services. Israel's military incursions produced the intended destruction but also encouraged a large number of new converts enraged by what the Israelis had done and fearful for the lives and well-being of their families and friends. Hezbollah and Hamas offered them a way of resisting and, when the fighting had ended, provided major funding for reconstruction at the grassroots level.

Our experience in Iraq has many parallels. Defeat of Saddam Hussein by our military was rapid, but we made lots of mistakes and were unable to win the peace because we were unable to address specific human needs at the local level. When neither the US military nor the Iraqi government were able to control violence, people looked to private sectarian militias to provide security and protection.

The lesson we must learn, then, is that conflict in the twenty-first century is broader than war, and the tools at our disposal must be broader than the US military. There are no quick fixes for us, but there are obvious places to start.

The United States used to have a very positive image in the world. Under the Marshall Plan after World War II, we provided aid and support to help reconstruct a devastated Europe and generated friendship and respect from the people of Europe and their governments. When Europe became self-sufficient, we provided food, healthcare, economic aid, and technical support to third-world countries, but primarily to keep them away from Soviet influence. Foreign aid was a significant component of our national budget until 1982, when our government decided to discontinue almost all of it, except for assistance to Israel and Egypt. Now, our foreign aid props up friendly governments and supports US contractors, who frequently do not speak the local language or understand their culture and values; who often take jobs away from indigenous workers; who associate primarily with other Americans; and who create disgruntlement among natives by frequenting the finest restaurants and hotels that the local people cannot afford. Too often, the ugly American presence is resented rather than appreciated by the people in need.

For most people in the world, their overriding desire is to have a better life for themselves and their families. Who runs the country, whether it is a democracy or not, is of lesser consequence as long as they feel safe and secure, live well according to their standards, have a sense of accomplishment, maintain good health, and enjoy life. Our message to the people of the world should be that we want to help them reach these goals. Indeed, we have done some things well. Our aid to tsunami victims in Sumatra and Sri Lanka, as well as earthquake victims in Pakistan, demonstrated the best that America can provide. Many nongovernmental organizations are highly regarded in other parts of the world, and the US Peace Corps has had a large positive overseas impact for a small expenditures of funds.

Indeed, a much-enlarged Peace Corps may be the appropriate agency to begin rebuilding America's moral authority abroad while unifying Americans at home. Most Americans would like to see us regain the admiration and respect of the rest of the world. This kind of program would naturally generate political support from liberals, but it is also a direction that would appeal to many on the religious right. Not too long ago, the head of the Christian Coalition of America resigned because the organization was focusing too much on gay marriage and abortion, and not enough on poverty, suffering, and health needs of people throughout the world. Furthermore, many young Americans today are seeking ways in which they can improve the world and would like to feel that their commitment could make a difference.

The potential lessons of the Iraq experience are many, but what this war tells us about the evolution of conflict is clear: war has changed and the instruments we need to ensure American security have changed too. Those fighting the war on terror must recognize and address the conditions that produce more terrorists. America must recommit to individual human security and become an agent for a better life throughout the world. That was the genius of the Marshall Plan in Europe, and it is a lesson for today as well.

It Takes a Country to Fight a War

Stephen A. Cheney

In the spring of 2003, our military demonstrated that it is unequaled at traditional warfare. Our forces performed superbly in taking down Saddam Hussein's government quickly and with relatively few casualties. But the uncoordinated efforts to rebuild Iraq have fallen well short of the mark. This is a monumental task that, regrettably, has principally fallen to the Department of Defense, and the shortcomings of this effort should serve as a lesson that wars of national liberation require strong interagency coordination.

The reconstruction response should incorporate significant contributions from many departments and agencies, including the Departments of State, Education, Treasury, and Energy. Our military forces are not adequately resourced—or prepared—to solely rebuild a country that is the size of California with a population of some 25 million.

In 2000, candidate George W. Bush said that US troops should not participate in nation-building. They should only, he said, fight and win the nation's wars. But President George W. Bush launched two of the biggest reconstruction and stabilization missions that the

United States has undertaken since World War II. In that war, President Roosevelt successfully coordinated and directed a national response to a geopolitical struggle. Today, we are involved in a vastly more complex, asymmetrical, unpredictable conflict—but we have not responded with a coherent strategy.

The lesson to be learned—and relearned—here is that all elements of national power must be employed when the nation's security is at risk. In order for our president to more fully harness and focus all of the capabilities of the United States government, perhaps a new interagency process is needed. The combatant commanders and the Joint Staff have in-depth contingency plans for a multitude of possibilities, but this level of preparation and response is not resident across government agencies (known as the *interagency* in Washington parlance)—but it should be.

The widely reported need, in 2007, to force some State Department diplomats to work in Iraq or face possible dismissal triggered strong emotions at the State Department, where the last such involuntary assignments occurred during the Vietnam War. A State Department spokesman said that more than fifteen hundred staffers had served in Iraq voluntarily since the US embassy in Baghdad opened in 2004 and that 94 percent of the department's Iraq jobs are filled, but the uproar raised questions about the sincerity of those who are—or are perhaps not—willing to serve in wartime. Or could it be that a number of citizens, including some at State, don't consider this "war" to be of such importance as to warrant their involvement or sacrifice?

Iraq, since 2003, has seen energy shortages, a lack of banks, a cash economy, and huge refugee flows. These have never been problems best solved by the Department of Defense. If this were truly a war and a threat to our nation's vital interests, then why have we not brought all the necessary resources to bear?

I believe it takes a country to fight a war, and our country—particularly the interagency—has not stepped up to the plate.

Rebalancing Our National Power

Joseph J. Collins

Extracting lessons from the war in Iraq is a difficult task. As Henry Kissinger has reminded us, history teaches by analogy and not by maxim. The study of Iraq will not yield any universally applicable lessons for the next president. In war and crisis management, context was, is, and always will be king.

To compound the problem, the war in Iraq is not over. Compare the hopeless summer of 2006 with the much brighter fall of 2008 in Iraq. Has the surge strategy put in motion qualitative, permanent improvements, or is it just a bright interlude before another violent storm? We don't know the answer to that question—and many others—about the outcome of the conflict. In all likelihood, Iraq and Afghanistan will be major issues past the 2012 election.

To contemplate preliminary lessons, we should consider the phases of the war in Iraq that have been completed. Although many participants have not yet given their accounts, we can make tentative judgments about the planning phase, the conventional attack, and our initial efforts at restoring stability to Iraq.

Much ink has been spilled on the foibles of our

planning process. Many journalists and scholars have pointed out that we had a good battle plan but inadequate plans for the day after. While the forces on hand were adequate for combat, they were inadequate for stability operations and not at all prepared for the insurgency that their numerical weakness and subsequent policy errors helped to create.

While the entire US policy leadership had agreed in March 2003 that we had to find the Iraqi equivalent of a Karzai and "put an Iraqi face" on the endeavor, we abandoned that effort in favor of a formal occupation. Despite valiant civil and military efforts, that formal occupation poured gasoline on the fires of insurgency.

Moreover, while Iraq was job one for the Bush administration after 2003, it took four years to give its commanders the manpower and to develop the operational charter they needed to make meaningful progress. The Bush team compounded those errors by funding the war through deficit spending.

All of this is spilt milk, some of which has been sopped up by the skill and determination of Americans on the ground in Iraq, beginning with General Petraeus and Ambassador Crocker. We should not, however, be complacent. The early phases of the war in Iraq exposed numerous decision-system or organizational problems that the president and Congress ignore at their own peril.

First, we need an interagency planning and decision mechanism for complex contingencies. Military plans should follow national plans, not vice versa. We also need new methods of deploying personnel and capabilities from the agencies of government beyond the Department of Defense. The interagency will provide unity of effort in executing national policy in the complex contingencies that are inevitable over the next decade.

Second, civil and military agencies must be better prepared for stability operations. The State Department has been given the lead for reconstruction and stabilization, but has not been adequately manned or funded for the job. Indeed, the overall organizational and fiscal weaknesses of the State Department and the US Agency for International Development (USAID) have become a critical impediment to US policy in all of its dimensions. We have to rebalance our national power.

In a similar vein, while our diplomats must become more expeditionary, our military must learn to think more in terms of the dynamics of irregular warfare, where victory doesn't come after a thunder run or a battlefield surrender. In 2005, the leadership of the Department of Defense put preparation for stability operations on par with a preparation for combat. State, Defense, and USAID have also made considerable efforts to learn about the political and military aspects of insurgency. The president and secretary of defense must follow through on these important efforts.

Third, in Iraq and other aspects of the war on terrorism, the United States has been hobbled by its inability to craft coherent messages and to explain its policies. We need to get better at public information, information operations, and public diplomacy. That effort cannot start at the State Department; it must begin in the White House. The president and his senior staff must coordinate our message and enhance the soft power of the United States.

Finally, the wars in Iraq and Afghanistan offer contrasting lessons in legitimacy. As our weak coalition in Iraq devolved into an Iraqi-American duet, the war in Afghanistan, with its higher level of legitimacy, has become NATO's war with over half of the fighting being done by US allies. Unlike the war in Iraq, there are almost no calls to end our support to Afghanistan, an ally that has only been supported by the United States but never occupied by it. The lesson here is simple: while it may be necessary to go it alone, the price for doing so is high and may well become greater over time. The only thing worse than fighting with allies is fighting without them.

America Needs a New Agency
to Help Failed States

Morton H. Halperin

America needs a new agency dedicated to helping failed states create and sustain the institutions needed to restore order and begin the process of reconstruction and development—one with the capacity to perform reconstruction responsibilities with an adequate budget, a mandate from Congress, and a career service. It also needs the authority to call up skilled manpower from our civilian society, as the military does.

After the US–led military victory in Iraq, the United States was as unprepared for what followed as it was in Bosnia, Haiti, and Kosovo, to name only three previous military interventions. In each case, during the months of planning for military intervention, there was no authoritative planning for what would need to follow. Many agencies planned for the reconstruction of each country, as the State Department did for Iraq. However, they did so without any clear mandate from the president and without a budget and a staff designed for these responsibilities.

The postwar tasks that need to be performed are by now well known. Most urgently, law and order need to be established. This means real police not military "police" who are trained for totally different functions, and it means quickly standing up an improvised criminal justice and prison system. Then—urgently—training needs to begin to create indigenous institutions to perform these and many other tasks, including drafting a constitution, running free and fair elections, and moving the economy forward.

The lesson of Iraq should be clear. The military does not have the capacity to perform these tasks and putting together an ad hoc reconstruction process is counterproductive and inefficient. The Bush administration tried to deal with this problem by setting up a coordinating mechanism in the State Department, but this solution is far from sufficient. We need a new agency for failed states.

This agency would be created by bringing together elements of existing agencies with operational capacity and budget authority, including the Office of Foreign Disaster Assistance and the Office of Transition Initiatives in the US Agency for International Development (USAID), part of the Refugee Bureau in the State Department and other functions scattered throughout State, the Justice Department, and other agencies.

If such an agency were created, it could begin planning for postcombat operations at the same time the military begins planning for its intervention. Knowing that it would be in charge of this process, the agency could recruit people in country and begin the process of training them for positions in the indigenous entities that would be urgently required, including local police. The agency could also call up and provide language and other training for police and other personnel to deal with the immediate aftermath of the intervention.

When the cold war began we recognized that we did not have the institutions that we needed to face this new threat and we created a host of new agencies, including the US Air Force, the Department of Defense, the Central Intelligence Agency, and, later, the US Agency for International Development and the US Information Agency. Since the cold war ended, and even since September 11, we have created only a single new agency—the Department of Homeland Security—despite profound changes in the international environment. Moving the boxes around to create a new department or creating a new coordinating mechanism is not a substitute for building a real agency with a career staff and a congressionally approved mandate and budget.

Indeed, we need several new agencies to address the emerging threats and opportunities of the twenty-first century, but the clearest requirement, well illustrated by the Iraq experience, is for a civilian agency to guide postconflict transition. We always think the current crisis will be the last, but it will not be, and we should not make this mistake again.

Debunking the Conventional Wisdom on Iraq

Benjamin H. Friedman and Christopher Preble

Conventional wisdom inside the Beltway holds that success could have been achieved in Iraq at a reasonable cost with more troops, better planning, and more cooperation among US government agencies. The policy recommendations that flow from these lessons aim to reform the national security bureaucracy so we will get it right the next time. But this view is wrong and dangerous. The Iraq debacle shows that we need a different national security strategy, not merely better tactics and tools to serve the current one.

By insisting that there was a right way to remake Iraq, we ignore the limits on our power that the enterprise has exposed and we risk repeating our mistake. Deposing Saddam Hussein was relatively simple, but creating a new state to rule Iraq was beyond our grasp. Maybe the United States can improve its ability to manage occupations, but the principal lesson Iraq teaches is to avoid them.

Conventional wisdom now says that the failures and errors in judgment can be attributed to poor planning. Better plans would have meant a larger invasion force, which would have prevented central authority in

Iraq from unraveling. If it had been operating from better plans, the Coalition Provisional Authority would not have pursued de-Baathification so aggressively, and it would not have let the Iraqi army collapse.

The planning for the occupation failed, the story goes, because government was uncoordinated and individual agencies were unprepared for unconventional war. Hence, various Washington think tanks have proposed to reform the national security bureaucracy. These proposals rely not only on faulty premises about Iraq, but also on undue faith in what the US government can achieve through planning and coordination.

The fact is, planning for the war was both plentiful and reasonably prescient. The problem was the Bush administration's unwillingness to use the plans. Accurate information about the likely postwar situation was available—it was either discarded or ignored. Ideology, combined with a healthy dose of wishful thinking and analytical bias, trumped expertise. No amount of bureaucratic rejiggering can make the president listen to the right people. The lesson here is not that the US national security establishment needs better planning, but that it needs better leaders. That problem is solved by elections, not bureaucratic tinkering.

The more important problem with the idea that planning could have saved Iraq is that it implies that proper organizational charts and meetings can stabilize broken countries and make order where there is none. This confuses a process with a policy, a bureaucratic mechanism with the power to establish a new political order. The trick is not having the right plans, but having the power to implement them. Americans never had that in Iraq; the power to conquer foreign countries is not the power to run them. There was not then and there is not now an American plan sufficient to solve Iraq's fundamental problem—the lack of popular support within Iraqi society for an equitable division of power.

Another reason Americans have struggled in Iraq is that nation-building is at odds with our national character. Whatever else changed after September 11, America remains unprepared for long-term military occupations. Neither the State Department nor the US Agency for International Development—technically part of State—is built to administer an empire. The department's budget is tiny because its aim is to relate to foreign nations, not to run them. When it comes to nation-building, brokering civil and ethnic conflict, and waging counterinsurgency, we are our own worst enemy, and that is a sign of our lingering common sense.

The lessons drawn from the war in Iraq should include caution about the limits of our power. The fetish for planning and reordering the national security establishment might produce some worthwhile changes, but if it makes it easier to wage wars to remake foreign societies, we will have learned nothing at all.

Beware of Dismantling States

Shibley Telhami

A few months before the Iraq war, I wrote a book, *The Stakes: America and the Middle East*, warning of its risks and noting that "the United States had the power to re-shuffle the deck in Iraq but not to determine where the cards will fall." I argued, among other things, that non-state terrorist groups like al Qaeda are empowered less by bad states than by the anarchic environment in the absence of states. While there are many lessons to be drawn from the Iraq war (about strategy, democracy promotion, planning, institutional coordination, public opinion, economic aid, and unilateralism, among many others), this lesson remains central.

Consider the stunning magnitude of failure of the Iraq war, measured against the stated aims: the United States, intent on keeping Iraq together and turning it into a democratic state, has probably spent more resources in that country than any state has ever spent on another in the history of the world.

All of Iraq's neighbors, for their own reasons, sought to avoid sectarianism and division in Iraq, even if many were suspicious of American intentions. Most of the major factions in Iraq, from their own perspectives, had interest in preventing civil conflict. Even the Kurds, who still aspire to independence one day, wanted to avoid a bloody civil war. All Arab states feared the breakup of Iraq, and Arab public opinion identified division of the country as one of their biggest concerns.

Yet, Iraq quickly descended into sectarian and tribal conflict; even if Iraq's society had not been highly sectarian, tribal and subsectarian divisions would have likely been accentuated—despite the strong Iraqi nationalism among most Iraqis. With all the improvements in the military and security environment in 2008, the degree of civil conciliation and the ability of the state to provide basic needs remained small; the future of a united, democratic Iraq is still in doubt.

Whether the security environment will continue to improve is also open to question, with or without the presence of American forces. Even if it does, it will likely come at a heavy cost. Either the need for American forces will continue to be essential to maintain stability in the country, or, in the presence of strengthened Iraqi military and security forces, these establishments will likely dominate politics in the country—as in many of the authoritarian states that were said to be the target of American policy. The Kurds are growing more autonomous by the day, even as the president of Iraq is a Kurd. That they aspire for independence is hardly a secret, even if they are unlikely to move in that direction recklessly.

Many critics of the Bush administration see the failure resting primarily with poor implementation. There is obviously that, on a bewildering scale, but no such large operation will ever take place without significant flaws and surprises. Even with the best American preparation, the odds against meeting the stated objectives in Iraq (creating a stable, prosperous, democratic Iraq) were high.

The problem is more fundamental: once the institutions of sovereignty are destroyed in any state, the challenge of quickly building a stable, let alone democratic, alternative grows considerably. In the absence of effective central authority, all it takes is a small, determined minority to prevent unity, maintain instability, and foil effective governance.

Despite the prevalence of troubled and troubling states, states remain the best candidates for maximizing international security. Confronting them is sometimes necessary, but dismantling them is dangerous. In the security arena, states remain the best enforcers of order. Many states need to be improved, others challenged and sometimes fought. But dismantling states remains one of the greatest dangers in our international system.

As we consider options toward other states not to our liking, Iraq should provide a helpful perspective. The next user of weapons of mass destruction is more likely to be a group like al Qaeda than any state. In its history, the United States has deterred the most ruthless and powerful states. Groups like al Qaeda are constrained only by the limits of their capability. Where there is absence of authority, they expand. Al Qaeda didn't exist in Iraq before the war, but thrived after the war began despite the presence of the most powerful army in the world.

Even in our weakened condition, the United States

retains the power to dismantle many troublesome states—
but we will never acquire enough power to replace them
to our liking.

PART FOUR

The Department of Defense at War

The Business of Defense Does Matter

Bill Owens

In retrospect, the list of lessons that could be learned from the Iraq experience leaves one somewhat stunned. How could so much have gone wrong?

A broader international mandate was likely possible, and we ought to have sought it. Once the initial campaign of shock and awe was over, we needed to better understand the vastly different culture we were working with in order to lead the country effectively. We should have immediately seized and controlled the tens of thousands of tons of munitions left in the Iraqi military magazines after we occupied Baghdad. Instead, these munitions have been used to create the improvised explosive devices that have killed and maimed far more Americans than were killed or wounded in the two wars we fought with Iraq's military forces in 1991 and 2003 combined. It is unconscionable that the US military did not have the needed stocks of body armor and up-armored vehicles. We should have deployed an effective multiagency effort, with the presence of US and international judicial, state, treasury, and intelligence agencies immediately after the military phase of operations. We could have employed lessons from the German experience with the East German military after the fall of the Berlin Wall and left the Iraqi military in place with a new set of goals that were secular and acceptable to the coalition. We should have had most of our troops immediately establish the security of the cities instead of searching for and killing insurgents in the outlying provinces.

The list goes on—too long to be explained as a unique coincidence of leadership personalities, errors in judgment, hubris, and bad luck. It points to deeper, systemic flaws within an institution that has not kept up with other American institutions: the Department of Defense.

The contrast with American business processes is striking. In a time when US legislative and regulatory agencies like the Securities and Exchange Commission have been putting so much effort into making our traditional businesses more accountable and attentive to shareholder interests, why have we not held the Department of Defense to the same standards and reviews? At a time when we are expanding our defense expenditures to all-time highs, and when the value of the dollar is in long-term decline, why are we not making the connection between the discretionary spending taking place in this account and the collapse of the dollar? How much bang for our buck did we get from our investments of the past decade for this new-world kind of crisis, which we arguably should have seen coming?

We have spent hundreds of billions of dollars on this war, and trillions in the preceding ten years building the military that fights it now. What are the forces that drive this process, and who is accountable for the capability, or lack thereof, that we have built over the years? For the resultant inefficiencies? For the loss of life (both American and Iraqi)? Specifically, who is responsible for the lack of preparation for the battle against terrorism that put the United States in a position from which we may not completely recover for decades?

I suggest that this is all about the business of American war fighting, and it is a business that is in trouble. It is not giving its stockholders—the American public and our sons and daughters who put their lives on the line—what they expect and deserve. Why is this?

Despite good intentions and good people, the business lacks transparency and accountability. I'm not talking specifically about defense contractors. I'm talking about the Department of Defense. It often cloaks its decisions and its rationale in unwarranted secrecy. The processes it uses to derive and implement them are obscure, driven by the esoteric and parochial interests of different military services, congressional districts, and defense contractors. Its congressional "board of directors" and its civilian management with direct experience in the military are shrinking. And it is slow, very slow, to change.

So, the Department of Defense invests in the past, not the future, and measures the value of its investments against the standards of an era that the world has left behind. Its investment accounts—how much it spends and on what—are out of line with the present and future.

The truth is, we should invest in the increased jointness that will bring synergy to our approach to fighting new world threats. These threats do not come from Russia or China and do not require substantial numbers of bombers, targeted nuclear weapons (where perhaps a hundred is enough), many dozens of nuclear submarines, fast carriers, or the extravagance of each of the four services having its own air force.

We should be using our resources to abandon the legacy of military bases for each of the fifty states. Indeed, it is remarkable that there continues to be no joint force bases. Yet, one can find several locations in the United States where at least two services have very large bases in the same location, at significant taxpayer cost.

Additionally, we need to move away from cold war production lines and unduly sustained defense contractors. It is not a time to cancel a few billion-dollar programs— the kinds of cuts that get the attention of the press. It is time to transform hundreds of billions of dollars of outdated legacies, both programmatic and cultural.

Instead, we ought to use our investments to expand the use of revolutionary commercial technology such as high-bandwidth digital communications, GPS devices, radio-frequency identification, and unmanned aerial vehicles. Did each soldier on the streets of Baghdad have an ability to see his local battlefield in the way this technology and new doctrine might have allowed? We must ensure that, in the future, our forces on the ground and in the air are provided with the greatest capabilities possible. We must ensure that we spend enough, as measured by a percentage of the total military budget, on C4ISR (command, control, communications, computers, intelligence, surveillance, and reconnaissance). These systems of systems can provide an umbrella-like view of the battlefield for an individual soldier or marine.

In the largest business in the world, it is critical to balance the pieces, rationalize the individual businesses, reduce or eliminate the unprofitable pieces, like those mentioned above, and transfer enough resources to well-understood requirements, such as mobile armored vehicles and C4ISR, and in sufficient quantity and quickly enough to matter.

Efforts over the last fifteen years to address these issues failed, in part or in whole, and these failures help explain how so much could go so wrong in Iraq. Unfortunately, the pernicious effects of mismanaging our defense business are not limited to Iraq.

The US defense budget stands at more than $500 billion a year, and is at least ten times that of the next largest in the world. It is the largest discretionary part of the total US budget and is directly linked to what has happened to the value of the dollar versus other currencies in the world. We could have a stronger, more relevant military if we cut defense by as much as $200 billion each year and invested those resources instead in US education or engagement programs around the world, or sustainable energy solutions such as clean coal. We could even look to taxpayer refunds. Such a policy would change the value of our currency compared to the euro and Chinese renminbi. Many of us living overseas can attest that this would help the competitiveness of American businesses.

In the business world, we look at the efficient use of resources to sustain and grow our market positions. One can question some of the basic parameters—or Key Performance Indicators—of the Department of Defense.

For example, on average, US forces deployed to Iraq have accounted for less than one-tenth the total number of forces in the US military. While we talk of overdeployment—and it is absolutely true for those brave troops who are in the deployable units that they are overdeployed—the grand majority of our forces (active duty, reserve, and National Guard) have not been deployed to Iraq, or have been deployed for only a small percentage of the time.

Although the navy and air force are unlikely in the next two or three decades to be as central to our national security strategy or to our war-fighting capability, it is likely, in the budget battles of the Pentagon, defense contractors, and Congress, that they will benefit as much or more than the US Army and Marine Corps from the lessons learned in Iraq and Afghanistan. The case will likely be made for attractive, capital-intensive airplanes and ships, and for readiness to combat a rising China or Russia, rather than for the people-heavy land forces to fight the war on terrorism. This outcome would not serve our citizen shareholders well.

Having served in the US Navy for thirty-four years, I have a special admiration and respect for the men and women of our four services. The American people provide a military with modern-day patriots. I served with them for all of my years in the military, and we are reminded every day of the very special, indeed exceptional, bravery we see from them around the world. We are, as a nation, blessed to have them, and should be proud to stand in their shadow as they take the best of our will and spirit to every corner of the globe, not questioning our political leaders, but serving our country with all of their capability. We owe it to them—and to the country as a whole—to learn the lessons of Iraq very carefully. A strong military should not be measured by how much we spend, but by the capability (for the expected missions) that we provide.

The lesson from the Iraq experience, then, is that running this most important defense business is a matter requiring the most dedicated political, defense, and business leadership by both civilian and military leaders. The business of defense does matter, and significant changes are required if we are to avoid repeating these mistakes.

The Undisciplined Pentagon Budget

Gordon Adams

One of the hidden consequences of Iraq is the impact that funding the war has had on the defense budget and planning system. Although few have acknowledged this reality, the lack of fiscal and planning discipline has caused this system to spin completely out of control. As a result, although future budget projections that appear relatively flat are causing concern in the Pentagon, the reality is that defense spending has grown way beyond any sensible requirement driven by any sense of strategy.

In 2008, President Bush asked Congress for $515 billion for defense in 2009—a figure that dramatically understates actual defense spending. When Iraq, Afghanistan, and the Department of Energy's defense functions are added, the United States will spend approximately $710 billion on defense in 2009. In 2002, the US defense budget was less than half that amount, $335 billion.

For the last seven years, emergency supplemental appropriations were the way out of the budget squeeze. In 2009, approximately 25 percent of defense spending will be classified as emergency funding. Now, the Department of Defense (DOD) wants to make this emergency spending part of the base budget, regardless of what happens in Iraq and Afghanistan. The chairman of the Joint Chiefs of Staff, Admiral Mullen, has asked that the Pentagon be guaranteed at least 4 percent of US gross domestic product. He has done so without strategy statement, mission description, or statement of requirements. He simply asserts that defense deserves a set share of the economy.

Indeed, the defense planning process is now encouraging this trend. The Bush administration announced its intention to add 92,500 permanent troops to the ground force—and then-candidate Barack Obama endorsed it. Here, too, no strategic justification has been provided. But planners know that the size of the force drives the rest of the budget. So, as the enlarged ground force ripples through DOD's planning and budgeting system, it will increase the pressure for more infrastructure investment, more training, more education, more operating funds, and, inevitably, more equipment. This is the consequence of how we have funded the Iraq war.

For the last nine budgets, from fiscal years 2001 to 2009, the share of overall defense resources coming through emergency supplemental funding has grown. Emergency supplementals are not like the regular budget, though they buy many of the same things: people, operations, and equipment. They don't get the same scrutiny and they don't go through the Pentagon's planning, programming, and budgeting process where they are scrubbed against the regular budget, with ceilings and trade-offs and the need for strategic, mission, and requirements justifications. Congress, too, devotes little time to examining emergency supplemental requests.

Over the years, DOD and the services have stuffed their supplementals with requests that don't fit the regular budget and are not really about Iraq: modular brigades for the army, increased end strength, certain aircraft systems. Indeed, to the Pentagon, supplemental funding and regular funding have become fungible.

Some will argue that this is wartime and the troops must be supported. But this is an argument without precedent. A Congressional Research Service review of how past administrations used supplemental budgets shows that using them to fund combat operations for seven years is unique. In Korea and Vietnam, war funding became an integral part of defense planning after a year or two, not a free good outside the regular budget.

It will be hard to restore discipline to the defense budget and planning system. The correction must begin with unexamined questions: What are we growing budgets for? What are the future strategies, requirements, and missions for which we are planning? And what is the straight line (not the rhetorical one) that ties them to a given sum of money?

Once we have the answers to these questions, we may find that we are overspending on defense and underspending on diplomacy and foreign assistance. Yes, our military is adaptable, capable, and flexible, but today it is overextended, not just in Iraq, but in its overall mission. It is deeply encroaching on territory that belongs to our diplomats and development programs—subsidizing foreign governments, building political institutions overseas, and providing foreign aid. And while many analysts and political commentators believe that US leadership in the world can be measured by an enormous defense budget, projecting military power as the leading edge of our international engagement has brought about a rising hostility to US foreign and security policy.

The lesson of Iraq, then, is that it is time to reexamine our strategy and our missions (and who performs them), and then look at the requirements, not the other way around. From operations and maintenance spending, where annually the United States spends $115,000 per soldier versus about $50,000 a decade ago, to procurement, where per-unit hardware costs are spiraling out of control, the Pentagon's absence of budget discipline is costing Americans billions of dollars that may be better spent elsewhere.

It is well past time to take a good, hard look at our national security strategy, forces, and equipment needs. And it is time to recognize, as Iraq has amply demonstrated, that leading with our military chin is getting us in trouble. It is even getting our forces in trouble as they try to adapt to missions that belong elsewhere in the government. It is time to recognize that we need all the tools in the tool kit of statecraft, which means rightsizing the military and reforming and building our civilian capability. Iraq has sent the system tasked with balancing these needs out of control and our security may be paying the price.

Broken Contract:
The Limits of the All-Volunteer Army

Lawrence J. Korb

One of the lessons of Iraq is that our nation's all-volunteer army (AVA) has suffered significant long-term damage waging an extended war it was not designed to fight.

When the Nixon administration ended the draft and switched to the all-volunteer force (AVF) in 1973, the service most affected was the army. For all practical purposes, in the period of conscription that lasted from 1948 to 1973, the army was the only service that had to rely on the draft to fulfill its manpower needs. (The marines had to draft small numbers in the waning years of Vietnam and the navy took in conscripts briefly in the mid-1950s.)

The AVA was to have four components: a comparatively small active force; a strategic reserve consisting of the Army National Guard and US Army Reserve, which would serve as a bridge to conscription if the nation became involved in a long war; a large pool of draft registrants who could be activated quickly; and private contractors who would take over mundane support functions like food service and routine maintenance.

This structure had two advantages. First, it held down costs. Even though the size of the active army was reduced, it still was the largest service and thus had the largest payroll. And with the creation of the AVF, the hidden tax of conscription ended and the cost of each soldier rose substantially. Second, a smaller force made it easier for the army to recruit sufficient numbers of high-quality personnel.

After getting off to a rough start, the AVA became a great success. By the mid-1980s, the active duty army was made up of high quality men and women. The guard and reserve were better trained and equipped than ever. Private contractors had assumed many of the routine support functions freeing up soldiers for combat missions. And after being discontinued briefly during the mid-1970s, draft registration was reinstituted and accepted by young men as part of becoming an adult.

The AVA performed very well in the Gulf War. Tens of thousands of guard and reserve personnel were activated to support the hundreds of thousands of soldiers deployed to the gulf. Private contractors provided food service and routine maintenance behind the lines and accounted for about 10 percent of those deployed there. Since the war lasted only thirty-seven days and the ground war only a hundred hours, there was no need to reinstitute the draft and the reserves were demobilized after about six months.

The second Gulf War—the invasion and occupation of Iraq in 2003—is another story altogether. To maintain its troop levels in Iraq (as well as Afghanistan), the army has had to violate its social contract with its active and reserve soldiers, use the guard and reserve as an operational rather than a strategic reserve, and rely on private contractors to perform military missions.

According to this social contract, active duty soldiers should get two years between one-year deployments and reserves should not be activated more than one year out of six. In the Iraq war, combat brigades have been lucky to get one year between deployments of fifteen months in Iraq. Many guard units have been activated several times since 2001. These reserve units are essentially rotating with active units in maintaining force levels in Iraq and Afghanistan.

The results of conducting this long war with an all-volunteer army have been devastating for the army and the country. To meet its needs, the active duty army has had to lower its educational and aptitude standards to unprecedented levels; raise the age for enlistment to forty-two; shorten enlistments to as little as 15 months; and give bonuses of up to $70,000 for new recruits and up to $150,000 to keep soldiers in. Even with these steps, the army has had to grant moral waivers (including those for felony convictions) to more than 10 percent of its new recruits. West Point graduates are leaving the service in numbers not seen in thirty years, leaving the army short thousands of captains.

Private contractors outnumber military personnel in Iraq and have had to take on military missions. When performing these missions, some contract personnel have used force so indiscriminately that they have undermined the counterinsurgency strategy.

All of this could have been avoided if the Bush

administration had invoked the third pillar of the AVF; that is, reinstate the draft to relieve the strain on the other three pillars. The question should be asked: if keeping some 200,000 troops in Iraq and Afghanistan for more than five years is not enough to activate the draft, then what is? How much damage to the AVA will our political leaders tolerate before dipping into the pool of draft registrants?

One Team, One Fight

Claudia Kennedy

The debate about the role of women in combat has been settled—permanently. The myopic view that sought to anchor the role of women in an operational no-man's-land has been rightly ignored in order to build the most effective army possible. The dysfunctional policies that reduced army readiness and imposed unwise and unwarranted restrictions on the full use of every soldier's talents have been thoroughly discredited.

We're not debating anymore whether women in combat are as effective as men. Instead, our focus is on the entire army team. Is the army effective? That is the appropriate question.

It turns out that the role of women in combat is far more than a domestic issue—it is of consequence in matters of our national security and also in international security. Because the security of our nation is deeply affected by international influences, we cannot judge the effectiveness of our security without reference to the security of others. So it is with judging the effectiveness of women as soldiers—it cannot be assessed in isolation. The effectiveness and readiness of the entire team is what ultimately matters.

The old, tired discussions about upper-body strength, foxhole hygiene and hormones, and pejorative arguments, such as "who will have the babies?" have simply been forgotten in the face of perfectly ordinary military performance by women in uniform and by the men with whom they serve. To call women's performance as soldiers ordinary is no slight. Rather, it avoids the tendency to attribute special qualities to women's service or require that they exhibit extraordinary skills to be considered acceptable. Women did not have to perform better than men for this argument to be settled, so superlatives are not needed.

The point of the army's personnel and operational policies is to maximize army readiness and to create the most effective army possible. The truth is, the way women have been assigned and are performing in Iraq and Afghanistan represents a sea change in army personnel policy. Admittedly, this is the product of necessity more than intention, but the results cannot be denied.

What we have learned in Iraq, among numerous other lessons, is that the role of women in combat is now resolved. It is years after the debate was settled operationally that we have now resolved the debate politically. Women in uniform, men in uniform—all part of the same fabric. It is, after all, one team, one fight.

Civil-Military Relations after Iraq

Frank G. Hoffman

The most important lesson to be drawn from the protracted war in Iraq is the importance of effective civil-
military relations to policy decision making. We have
painfully relearned one of Carl von Clausewitz's oft-
quoted but rarely absorbed comments: "The first, the
supreme, the most far-reaching act of judgment that
the statesman *and* commander have to make is to establish...the kind of war on which *they* are embarking."[1]
This supreme judgment highlights the complexity of
key relationships between civilian leaders and military
commanders that are crucial to strategic decision making and the development of sound and actionable policy.
History is replete with cases of strategic defeat attribut-
able to limited policy discussions and dysfunctional relationships between the statesman and his generals.[2] Iraq
has added another footnote to this litany.

Civil-military relations are too often conflated with
power or control. In the United States, civilian *control*
is not at issue, but civil-military relations—properly
defined—*is*. Civilian control is constitutionally grounded
in America. But civil-military relations and effective strategic performance are not. This is because the interface

between policy leaders and military officers entail a far broader and less structured problem. Arriving at sound policy requires discipline, deliberate process, and continuous discourse. Ultimately, it is about the interchange of viewpoints and the production of effective strategies for the use of the military instrument.

Properly included within a broad definition of civil-military relations is the mutual respect and understanding between civilian and military leaders, and the exchange of candid views and perspectives in the decision-making process. It is not about dictation from policy master to supplicants and servants. It is about the tenor of the dialogue and the quality of the resulting policy decisions and strategic plans.[3]

American strategic culture artificially divides policy from military operations. Dr. Samuel Huntington, in his *The Soldier and the State*, codified this predominant—albeit flawed—model into a theory of civil-military relations that gives the military leadership clear autonomy over the professional military sphere.[4] The ramifications of this model were played out during the last two conflicts that the United States entered with fairly predictable results. There is no separate sphere or clear demarcation between policy, strategy, and operations; in fact, what is needed is a constructive bridge. But in Iraq's planning cycle, our statesmen and commanders failed to properly determine the kind of war that they were embarking upon, failed to work together to develop and implement strategies to achieve desired policy, and clearly failed to properly adapt policy and strategy as the conflict evolved.

The current narrative pins fault principally on President Bush's civilian policy advisors for the war's poor planning and its attendant costs. The president admitted to being "a product of the Vietnam world" and loath to influence decisions about the use of the military. He recognized there is a very fine line between setting strategy and micromanaging combat.[5] He consciously sought to avoid constraining his generals or impacting their ability to win the war and avoided getting involved in details.[6] But the president greatly valued personal loyalty and surrounded himself with people who placed a premium on conformity over deliberate and transparent process. This was an environment in which dissent was uniformly discouraged.[7]

Most of the opprobrium in this tragedy is saved for Donald Rumsfeld. The secretary of defense made it clear from his arrival that he wanted to be in control; he was extremely sensitive to challenges to civilian authority.[8] He felt that control over the military had been allowed to slip during the Clinton administration and he vowed to shake things up. He came to the Pentagon armed with an agenda to transform the US military and make it more agile and lean. He had qualms with the existing "Clinton Generals" and believed the Joint Staff was useless.[9] He challenged the status quo at every turn and was a legendary micromanager. He insisted on approving and challenging the Joint Staff's process for deploying military units during Operation Iraqi Freedom (OIF). The uniformed military resented the imposition of his untested conceptions of future military fights into current operations and war plans. Comparisons to Vietnam and the meddling of Robert S. McNamara were rife. This was an "extraordinary degree of micromanagement that frustrated and enraged the military."[10]

The flip side of the indictment involves the professional competence of senior military advisors. They are accused of having failed to provide candid military counsel because they were intimidated yes-men, or because they failed to recognize the complexity of the war. This line of thinking concludes that Rumsfeld got what he wanted: a compliant military that would do his bidding. Collectively, the Joint Chiefs had "surrendered" to Rumsfeld, with one member admitting that "The Joint Chiefs have been systemically emasculated."[11]

The same charge is levied against the theater commander, General Tommy Franks, during the planning cycle for both Operation Enduring Freedom (OEF) and OIF. Some observers claimed that General Franks deferred to Rumsfeld too much and failed to represent military viewpoints with any authority.[12] This deference allowed Rumsfeld's perspectives on force levels to prevail and set up the troop shortfalls that contributed partly to OIF's difficulties. Rumsfeld put the Joint Staff and Franks's headquarters under constant pressure to conduct that campaign with smaller force levels, and he and his staff offered unrealistic proposals that consumed time that would have been better spent on Phase IV, the postconflict period.[13] The result was a plan for a great battle fought according to American preferences, but not a solid strategy for gaining US policy aims in the postwar period.

At the heart of the narrative is a long-standing debate about the role of the US military in policy and political matters. One myth embedded in the American way of war is the notion that there should be a clear and inherent division of labor between civilian and military spheres of responsibility. Under this construct, civilian leaders should set forth clear policy aims and then avoid close supervision of plans or the conduct of war by military commanders. On one side, civilians are responsible for assigning political objectives and end states, and the military is wholly responsible for strategy, military objectives, and war fighting. This myth is partly based on Huntington's normative theory, which claims that military professionalism and civilian control are enhanced by acknowledging an autonomous sphere for military professionals.[14]

But history and our own Iraq experience suggest that strategic performance is not enhanced by separate and too often isolated spheres. How do we resolve the dilemma? How are the responsibilities for policy development, decision making, and supervision divided among civilians and military professionals? Dr. Eliot Cohen's *Supreme Command* offers a historically grounded answer. Cohen argues that each side provides its unique experience and perspective to the crisis at hand in what he termed an "unequal dialogue." Based upon four case studies, he concluded that great statesmen do not accept an artificial dividing line that separate the two spheres. They do more than merely define policy. His model statesmen were masters of detail who were intimately involved in planning and supervising, always "querying, prodding, suggesting, arbitrating," and occasionally overruling their military advisors. They did more than merely offer guidance or goals; they selected commanders, fired

others, meddled when necessary, and drove the refine-
ment of strategies and plans until they were satisfied with
the logic linking the military plans to political aims.
Cohen recommends policymakers

> immerse themselves in the conduct of their wars no
> less than in their great projects of domestic legisla-
> tion; that they must master their military briefs as
> thoroughly as they do their civilian ones; that they
> must demand and expect from their military subor-
> dinates a candor as bruising as is necessary; that both
> groups must expect a running conversation in which
> although civilian opinion will not usually dictate, it
> must dominate; and that conversation will cover not
> only ends and policies, but ways and means.[15]

In short, tomorrow's policymakers need to ask hard questions about military proposals and actively participate in
the inherently difficult process of translating political
objectives into military plans. Military planners must
be challenged to ensure that everyone understands the
logic and grammar behind military plans. This process
requires military leaders have the moral courage to ask
the same about the ends of policy and the ramifications of
the total costs from their civilian masters. These running
conversations certainly do involve ways and means. The
melding of ends and means is a two-sided and interactive
process, as policy may have to be informed and adapted
by the limits of available and appropriate tools.[16]

 This was not true during the Vietnam conflict. The
"loose assumptions, unasked questions and thin analyses"

of the Johnson administration were not challenged. Johnson and McNamara were not willing to have the same sort of intellectual debate over assumptions, goals, and priorities with military advisors.[17] They cut out the Joint Chiefs from any meaningful discussion. The same appears to have been true for Iraq. There was no continuous dialogue or "running conversation" at the strategic level.[18] True, there was an intensive and prolonged conversation on the amount of the means being used, but rarely on the way in which those forces were to be applied. Here, Rumsfeld's powerful attention to detail was misplaced. There was little focus on the logic of the operation and how force was being employed.

Some academics want to revert to Huntington and suggest that civilian interference in Iraq is the proximate cause of our elongated campaign. Such arguments should be rejected. We need to displace a flawed theory of civil-military relations and accept the more historically grounded model that accounts for the overlapping and reciprocal interrelationships of ends, ways, and means that leads to strategic success.[19] Instead of allowing the military to retreat to a zone of professional autonomy but political autism, we need to establish new norms that set up expectations for a decision-making climate that encourages candid advice and the rigorous exchange of views and insights. It is the duty of civilian leaders, in all branches of government, to establish that climate, and it is the moral obligation of military professionals to honestly and clearly present their best advice in the planning process.

During 2002 and 2003, Pentagon civilian officials

failed to live up to the requirements for candor, collaboration, and cooperation. They did not appreciate the sworn obligation of military officers to provide their best professional counsel or the valuable insights of their experience. At the same time, senior military leaders failed to serve as a strategic bridge between policy and the actions on the ground. The focus on the rapid sprint to Baghdad reflects a warped understanding of campaigning and contributed to the difficult occupation and insurgency that followed. Nor did military leaders adapt quickly to the challenges that Iraq's protracted irregular content posed. There is enough fault to go around with respect to shoddy planning and unexamined assumptions in Iraq.

The management of the civil-military relationship is not merely a function of military subservience. It is also the purview of civilian leaders. Failure to shape the culture, codes, and character of the profession until war occurs is guaranteed to result in decreased strategic performance. Civil-military relations is a *critical* component of security policy, and any country that fails to consider the intense and interactive discourse that drives policymaking runs fairly considerable risks. We need to close the gap on what Colin Gray calls the "reciprocal ignorance" of two worlds that lack the perspective, background, and knowledge base to appreciate the other side.[20] This will require effort on both sides. Based on the growing complexity of conflict and the reality of US demographics, the potential for mutual ignorance is growing as fewer and fewer policy leaders will have direct exposure to military service and experience.[21]

Dr. Cohen once concluded, "the study of the relationship between the soldier and statesmen lies at the heart of what strategy is all about."[22] The development and implementation of effective policy and strategy, and civil-military relations, are inextricably linked. The decision making behind the US interventions in Afghanistan and Iraq underscores this conclusion. It also highlights the need for serious discussion. Unless efforts are made to rectify the components that constitute the entire relationship between the nation and its uniformed servants, expectations for improved performance are low. More fundamentally, expectations for greater volatility between the institutions of our government will be high. If we continue to neglect the nature of the unequal dialogue that constitutes the ultimate decision regarding war, we will continue to pay a high price.

Notes

1. Carl von Clausewitz, *On War*, Michael Howard and Peter Paret, ed. & trans. (Princeton, NJ: Princeton Univ. Press, 1986), 88 (emphasis added).

2. See my essay "History and Future of Civil-Military Relations, Bridging the Gaps," in Williamson Murray and Richard Hart Sinnreich, eds., *The Past as Prologue: The Importance of History to the Military Profession* (New York: Cambridge Univ. Press, 2006), 247–265; for modern history, see Peter D. Feaver, *Armed Servants: Agency, Oversight, and Civil-Military Relations* (Cambridge, MA: Harvard Univ. Press, 2003).

3. Andrew J. Bacevich, "Elusive Bargain: The Pattern of US Civil-Military Relations Since World War II," in *The Long War: A New History of US National Security Policy Since World War II* (New York: Columbia Univ. Press, 2007), 210.

4. For more on this issue, see Mackubin T. Owens, "Huntington at

50," *The Weekly Standard*, October 2007.

5. Bob Woodward, *Bush At War* (New York: Simon & Schuster, 2002), 145.

6. Ibid., 176.

7. Ron Suskind, *The Price of Loyalty* (New York: Simon & Schuster, 2004), 329.

8. Charles A. Stevenson, *SECDEF: The Nearly Impossible Job of Secretary of Defense* (Dulles, VA: Potomac Books, 2007), 178.

9. Bob Woodward, *State of Denial: Bush at War, Part III* (New York: Simon & Schuster, 2006), 38.

10. Ibid., 103–104.

11. Ibid., 404.

12. Woodward, *Bush at War*, 251. According to Woodward, Franks once chummed up to Rumsfeld on a VTC by responding, "Sir, I think exactly what my secretary thinks, what he's ever thought, what he will ever think or whatever he thought he might think."

13. Thomas Ricks, *Fiasco: The American Military Adventure in Iraq* (New York: Penguin, 2006), 42–43.

14. Samuel P. Huntington, *The Soldier and the State* (Cambridge, MA: Belknap Press, 1981), 83. "The essence of objective civilian control is the recognition of autonomous military professionalism."

15. Eliot A. Cohen, *Supreme Command: Soldiers, Statesmen, and Leadership in Wartime* (New York: New York Free Press, 2002), 206.

16. On the interplay between policy, politics, and war, see Antulio J. Echevarria II, *Clausewitz and Contemporary War* (New York: Oxford Univ. Press, 2007), 85–97.

17. George C. Herring, *LBJ and Vietnam: A Different Kind of War* (Austin: Texas Univ. Press, 1994), 13–16.

18. Cohen, *Supreme Command*, 206.

19. Hew Strachan, "Making Strategy: Civil-Military Relations after Iraq," *Survival* 48, no. 3 (October 2006): 71. If it ever was valid Strachan makes it clear that "Huntington's model of civil-military relations is proving profoundly dysfunctional to the waging of war in the twenty-first century."

20. Colin S. Gray, *Modern Strategy* (Oxford, UK: Oxford Univ. Press, 1999), 61.

21. Dr. John Hillen, "Servants, Supplicants, or Saboteurs: The Role of the Uniformed Officer and the Changing Nature of America's Civil-Military Relations," in Douglas T. Stuart, ed., *Organizing for*

National Security (Carlisle, PA: Army War College, 2000), 218.

22. Cohen, *Supreme Command*, xii.

PART FIVE

Conclusions

And to the Republic for Which it Stands

Gary Hart

The founders of the United States knew what they were doing when they created a republic. From their extensive knowledge of Athens and Rome, they knew a republic to be based on the sovereignty of the people, to involve civic duty, to demand resistance to the corruption of special interests, and to require a sense of the commonwealth. Equally important, they knew that, throughout history, a republic could not also be an empire.

Had we been more aware of our history and the culture of the republic, we could have avoided the temptations of empire the invasion of Iraq represented. Despite grand rhetoric about bringing democracy to the Middle East, it was clear from the outset that the architects of the Iraq invasion had in mind to make an American-friendly Iraq our political and military base in the region. And from that base we would bring contentious neighbors such as Iran and Syria to heel, promote our political and economic institutions and values throughout the region, and go a long way toward protecting Persian Gulf oil supplies.

As our European allies could have told us from their largely bitter experiences in the business of colonialism, it is not always so easy. There is, first of all, the requirement that the postinvasion government of the host nation remain friendly, that it tolerate a long-term American military presence and civilian oversight of its administration, and that it acquiesce in the use of its territory as an American fiefdom. The Iraqis had almost three decades of this experience with the British and it did not work out well for either party.

As happened in the Philippines during the Spanish-American War a century earlier, it has taken a five-year occupation of a hostile nation to remind ourselves of the price of empire and the reason why our founders were so adamant that we were and should remain a republic. In the long history of nations, one might observe that learning this lesson once every hundred years or so is acceptable, if it weren't for the costs and consequences: more than thirty thousand American casualties, the transformation of Iraq into a recruiting and training ground for terrorists, and the incalculable damage to American relations in the Islamic world and elsewhere.

Were the theory of winning a war on terrorism by invading every nation that harbored terrorists to be taken seriously, we would have been required to invade quite a lot of nations, including some very friendly to us. It is not so easy, and one suspects that those who concocted the grand imperial scheme for Iraq were never serious about this. Instead, they had other agendas they did not trust the American people enough to reveal.

We will have our hands full for quite some time trying to tame a tribal society in Afghanistan enough to keep al Qaeda at bay and the Taliban in its caves. The sooner we abandon the naive and dangerous imperial venture in Iraq, the sooner we can get on with it, and the sooner we can remind ourselves that we are not and never should be an imperial power and that we salute the flag of a republic.

No More Iraqs

James N. Miller Jr.

Although the final chapter on the Iraq war has not been written, it is already clear that one of the preeminent lessons will echo that of the Vietnam War: that is No More Iraqs. This bumper-sticker maxim, however, will have widely divergent interpretations. Some will probably be right, several will certainly be wrong, and for some it is simply too soon to tell.

The list of valid No-More-Iraqs lessons is the longest and the one that should be carried in the pockets of all would-be policymakers. It begins with the need for effective prewar planning, with an underscored notation that questionable single-source intelligence should never again be accepted. Nor should operational planning exclude the State Department and other civilian agencies with essential expertise. Nor should US leaders show disdain for key allies and then expect them to send troops to a war they believe ill advised. And never again should the secretary of defense minimize the forces allocated to an operation based on an unproven theory of military transformation.

With respect to the conduct of the war, and in particular its initial several years, the list continues with the No-More-Iraqs warning that no future secretary of defense should direct occupying forces not to intervene while looting and mayhem tilt a country toward chaos. Nor should the occupied state's remaining instruments of order and governance (the Iraqi army and the Baath Party) be disbanded without any replacement in sight. Nor should unwelcome assessments of the situation on the ground be dismissed or downplayed, thereby inhibiting rather than spurring necessary strategic adaptation as insurgency and civil war erupt. Individuals must not be selected for critical overseas positions based on party loyalty as opposed to professional competence. And never again should the Congress take a pass on conducting real oversight of a war.

In contrast with these pieces of distilled wisdom are three inappropriate No-More-Iraqs lessons that are already gaining unfortunate currency. First, some suggest that the United States should avoid promoting democracy abroad and should instead practice a foreign policy narrowly focused on vital American interests and in particular protecting the US homeland. However, a foreign policy that does not account for American values as well as interests will not be sustainable domestically or internationally. Thus, the question is not whether but *how* the United States should attempt to foster democracy abroad. Creating democracy by invading another country is at best a costly last-resort long shot. On the other hand, judiciously supporting indigenous democratic governments and movements is more likely to be sustainable and to succeed over the longer term.

Second and related, some will suggest that the US

military should focus solely on fighting and winning the nation's wars and once again reject missions that look suspiciously like nation-building. However, given that protecting American interests requires helping struggling nations provide security and good governance for their people, the US military must prepare for the missions it is likely to be asked to perform. And that will involve complex counterinsurgency and counterterrorism missions and a diverse array of stability operations much more often than the Desert Storm–type wars that some would prefer to fight.

Third and most broadly, to some No More Iraqs will mean no more wars of choice. Unfortunately, because terrorism, weapons of mass destruction, and the potential for genocidal violence will remain key parts of the strategic landscape, the United States will find occasions when it is necessary, and indeed just, to use military force, as it did, for example, in Afghanistan, against Iraq in the limited strikes of Desert Fox, and in Kosovo. The United States cannot and should not intervene at the drop of a hat, but it must be prepared to employ its military in order to protect American strategic interests when other tools of statecraft simply won't work.

Finally, No More Iraqs should mean a policy based on pragmatism and professionalism, rather than ideology and wishful thinking. If policymakers can just remember this last lesson—even if they forget or misplace the others—then they already stand a better chance of negotiating the treacherous shoals ahead in the formulation and execution of American foreign policy.

Iraq: Lessons Learned

James M. Ludes

The Iraq war has lasted longer and cost more than anyone predicted before the start of the conflict. Its cost in human life, in national wealth, and in the damage it has done to our moral authority in the world is staggering. The lessons we might draw from the experience are legion, but three are uppermost in my mind.

War is about the breaking of wills, not the breaking of armies. The United States Army and the United States Marine Corps raced to Baghdad in three weeks. But the war did not end. US forces smashed Saddam Hussein's armies. American pilots alone ruled the skies over Iraq. Our forces drove the Iraqi dictator underground—literally. They hunted down his former lieutenants, including his sons. They occupied his entire country. They inflicted grave losses on anyone who challenged them. They turned the country upside down looking for suspected weapons of mass destruction. Yet the violence never ceased. Much of it was an expression of long-contained sectarian violence. But much was armed resistance against US occupation.

Fundamentally, war is a political endeavor that once begun will persist as long as the will and means to resist remain. The next time a salesman for some future conflict promises a cakewalk, remember the Iraq war.

The truth is that war is full of the unanticipated and the unintended. Look at the Pentagon's prewar plans for dealing with casualties of biological or chemical weapons. Yet no soldier suffered from such ghastly weapons. No, the highest percentage of US casualties were victims of improvised explosive devices—artillery shells camouflaged along roadsides and detonated by cell phones, garage door openers, or wired triggers. US forces were not prepared for these weapons because there is no way to fully anticipate humanity's creativity for destruction.

When the United States went to war in 2003, few believed the conflict would drag on this long or take such a toll on our wealth and on the lives of so many young Americans. But history is full of conflicts that didn't go precisely as their architects had planned: consider our own war for independence, the Crimean War in the middle of the nineteenth century, and Iraq today. This lesson often seems to be dismissed in the rush to war, only to be relearned painfully in the bloody tribulations that follow. This uncertainty—historic and enduring as it is—should humble any policymaker contemplating the use of force, now and in the future.

Finally, the Iraq war should inspire all Americans to take a closer look at what passes for "strategy" in the public discussion of America's national security and demand better. Popular television programs on the half dozen military and history channels available on cable glorify push-button military solutions to incredibly complex challenges. The media, from talk radio and cable news to newspapers, meanwhile, pass entertainment off as news, forgetting that journalists should be skeptical reporters, not unthinking purveyors of (mis)information.

At the end of the day, the many failures in Iraq cannot be laid at the hands of any one person, or even a few people. This is our country, we are a democracy, and so these are our failures. For decades, the public's attention has drifted away from the serious discussion of national issues. Then, in the aftermath of the September 11 terrorist attacks, when real debate was warranted and the country's attention was focused like never before, any thoughtful challenge of presidential policy was dismissed as either disloyalty or the coddling of our enemies. Fear and intimidation stifled debate in the press and in Congress. Too few raised their voices in patriotic skepticism. Too few shrugged off the censorship of mass opinion to ask hard questions, demand a wiser course, and lead us to a better way. A disastrous war was the result.

As a Senate aide from 2002 to 2006, I had the solemn privilege to attend the burial of several Americans at Arlington National Cemetery. Few things focus the mind on the true cost of war more than standing quietly on the grass as a young widow and proud parents grieve and say their last good-byes. As a country, we owe it to them, and those they lost, to take seriously the effort to learn from this experience so that we gain wisdom—and from wisdom, strength.

CONTRIBUTORS

Gordon Adams is a professor of international relations at the School of International Service, American University, and a distinguished fellow at the Henry L. Stimson Center. From 1993 to 1997, he was associate director for national security and international affairs at the Office of Management and Budget, the senior White House official for national security budgets.

Thomas P. M. Barnett is a best-selling author and nationally known public speaker who has worked in national security affairs since the end of the cold war. He is senior managing director of Enterra Solutions, LLC, and author of *The Pentagon's New Map*. His most recent book is *Great Powers: America and the World after Bush*.

Rt. Rev. John Bryson Chane, DD, is the Episcopal bishop of Washington, DC, and Washington National Cathedral.

Brig. Gen. Stephen A. Cheney (US Marine Corps, Ret.) is a member of the American Security Project's board of directors and is the president of Marine Military Academy in Harlingen, Texas. Prior to that appointment he was chief operating officer for Business Executives for National Security. Cheney served over thirty years in the Marine Corps, including a tour as commanding general with the Marine Corps Recruit Depot, Eastern Recruiting Region in Parris Island, South Carolina.

Lt. Gen. Daniel Christman (US Army, Ret.) is a member of the American Security Project's board of directors. He is senior vice president for international affairs at the United States Chamber of Commerce. From 1996 to 2001, Christman was superintendent of the United States Military Academy at West Point. He has also served as president and executive director of the Kimsey Foundation. During his tenure with the US Army, he was the assistant to the chairman of the Joint Chiefs of Staff and represented the United States as a member of NATO's Military Committee in Brussels, Belgium.

Joseph J. Collins is a professor of strategy at the National War College and an adjunct professor in Georgetown University's Security Studies Program. A retired army colonel, he served from 2001 to 2004 as the deputy assistant secretary of defense for stability operations, where he was active in plans and policy for the war in Afghanistan, as well as in the initial planning for Operation Iraqi Freedom. Collins is a veteran of over a decade's service in the Pentagon and has taught at West Point, Georgetown, and Columbia universities. His many publications include books on Soviet policy toward Afghanistan, international relations theory, and US military culture. The thoughts expressed in "Rebalancing Our National Power" are his alone and are not meant to reflect government policy.

Bernard I. Finel is a senior fellow at the American Security Project (ASP), where he directs research on counterterrorism and defense policy. He is the lead author of ASP's annual report, *Are We Winning? Measuring Progress in the Struggle against al Qaeda.*

Benjamin H. Friedman is a research fellow at the Cato Institute and a PhD candidate in the Security Studies Program at MIT.

Robert Gallucci is dean of the Edmund A. Walsh School of Foreign Service at Georgetown University. He is a leading expert in US foreign policy and international efforts to stop weapons of mass destruction programs. His career with the US State Department included service on the first post–Gulf War arms inspection effort known as the UN Special Commission on Iraq and as the lead ambassador responsible for the negotiation of the 1994 Agreed Framework, which significantly impacted North Korea's nuclear weapons program.

V. Adm. Lee F. Gunn (US Navy, Ret.) is president of the American Security Project. He is also president of the Institute of Public Research at The CNA Corporation, a nonprofit corporation in Virginia. During his thirty-five-year career in the US Navy, he served as inspector general of the Department of the Navy; deputy chief of Naval Personnel; commander, Navy Personnel Command; commander, Amphibious Group Three; and deputy commander, Combined Task Force United Shield, protecting the withdrawal of UN forces from Somalia.

Morton H. Halperin is senior fellow at the Center for American Progress. Halperin served in the Johnson, Nixon, and Clinton administrations, most recently as director of the policy planning staff at the Department of State (1998–2001). From 1975 to 1992, Halperin directed the Center for National Security Studies, a project of the American Civil Liberties Union (ACLU), which sought to reconcile requirements of national security with civil liberties. From 1984 to 1992, he also directed the Washington office of the ACLU, where he was responsible for its national legislative program. Halperin has published a number of books, including *Bureaucratic Politics and Foreign Policy*, *The Democracy Advantage*, and *Protecting Democracy*.

Sen. Gary Hart is chairman of the American Security Project. He served Colorado in the US Senate and was a member of the Committee on Armed Services during his tenure. Hart was a candidate for the Democratic nomination for president in 1984, and more recently he was cochair of the US Commission on National Security in the 21st Century, otherwise known as the Hart-Rudman Commission, an effort that warned of the danger of attacks on US homeland. He also cochaired the Council on Foreign Relations task force on homeland security, which released a major report entitled "America—Still Unprepared, Still in Danger." He has been a visiting fellow and lecturer at Oxford University and is the author of *The Shield and the Cloak: The Security of the Commons*.

Lt. Col. Frank G. Hoffman (US Marine Corps, Ret.) is a retired marine infantry officer with a background in military theory and strategy. He is. a nonresident senior fellow with the Foreign Policy Research Institute (FPRI) in Philadelphia.

"Civil-Military Relations after Iraq" is an adaptation of a larger essay that appeared in the Summer 2008 issue of *Orbis*, FPRI's flagship foreign policy journal, and is printed with the gracious permission of FPRI.

Robert D. Hormats is vice chairman of Goldman Sachs International and a managing director of Goldman, Sachs & Co. He served as a senior staff member for international economic affairs at the National Security Council from 1974 to 1977, ambassador and deputy US trade representative from 1979 to 1981, and assistant secretary of state for economic and business affairs from 1981 to 1982. Hormats's numerous articles and publications include the recently released book *The Price of Liberty: Paying for America's Wars from the Revolution to the War on Terror.*

Lt. Gen. Claudia Kennedy (US Army, Ret.) was the first woman to achieve the rank of three-star general in the United States Army. She served as the senior intelligence officer for US Forces Command, deputy commanding general for the Army Intelligence Center and School, and completed her army career as the deputy chief of staff for intelligence. She is chair of First Star nonprofit corporation, working on behalf of children, and serves on the board of directors of the American Security Project.

Lawrence J. Korb is a senior fellow at the Center for American Progress and a senior advisor to the Center for Defense Information. Prior to joining the center, he was a senior fellow and director of national security studies at the Council on Foreign Relations. From July 1998 to October 2002, he was council vice president, director of studies, and holder of the Maurice Greenberg Chair. Korb served as assistant secretary of defense (Manpower, Reserve Affairs, Installations and Logistics) from 1981 through 1985. In that position, he administered about 70 percent of the defense budget. For his service in that position, he was awarded the Department of Defense Medal for Distinguished Public Service.

Steven Livingston is a professor of political communication in the School of Media and Public Affairs (SMPA) and holds a joint appointment in the Elliott School of International Affairs at the George Washington University. He is also a research professor in the Political Science Department and is a faculty associate in George Washington University's Space Policy Institute. Livingston's research and teaching focus on media, advanced information technology, and international affairs. He is also chairman of the board of the Public Diplomacy Institute, an organization within SMPA he cofounded. He is the author of *When The Press Fails: Political Power and the News Media from Iraq to Katrina*.

James N. Miller Jr. is senior vice president and director of studies at the Center for a New American Security, and co-author of *Phased Transition: A Responsible Way Forward and Out of Iraq*. He has served as deputy assistant secretary of defense in the Clinton administration, advisor to the Defense Science Board, senior professional staff member to the House Armed Services Committee, senior vice president of a private sector consulting firm, and in numerous academic positions over the past twenty-five years.

Lt. Col. John A. Nagl (US Army, Ret.) is president of the Center for a New American Security. A retired army officer, he fought in operations Desert Storm and Iraqi Freedom and helped write *The US Army/Marine Corps Counterinsurgency Field Manual.*

Arthur S. Obermayer is a scientist, businessman, and philanthropist who has aided in shaping US government policy. After receiving his PhD from MIT, he began and ran a high-tech company, which initially worked on underground nuclear weapons tests and then radically restructured itself into a chemical and pharmaceutical research corporation. Since selling his business to an Australian drug company, his attention has primarily been on critical issues involving the relationship of the United States to Russia, Israel, and Germany.

Adm. Bill Owens (US Navy, Ret.) is chairman and CEO of Hong Kong–based private equity investment group AEA Holdings ASIA and a managing director of AEA Investors. In a distinguished thirty-four-year US Navy career, Owens served most recently as vice chairman of the Joint Chiefs of Staff, the second-ranking military officer in the United States, where he had responsibility for the reorganization and restructuring of the armed forces in the post–cold war era. He has written more than fifty articles on national security and authored two books, *High Seas* and *Lifting the Fog of War.*

Paul R. Pillar is a visiting professor and member of the core faculty in the Security Studies Program at Georgetown University. Pillar has twenty-eight years of experience in the US intelligence community, most recently as national intelligence officer for the

Near East and South Asia. He is the author of *Negotiating Peace* and *Terrorism and US Foreign Policy*.

Christopher Preble is director of foreign policy studies at the Cato Institute. "Debunking the Conventional Wisdom on Iraq" is adapted from the Cato Policy Analysis "Learning the Right Lessons from Iraq."

Shibley Telhami is Anwar Sadat Professor for Peace and Development at the University of Maryland and nonresident senior fellow at the Saban Center of the Brookings Institution. An earlier version of "Beware of Dismantling States" appeared in the *Baltimore Sun* in 2006.

More thought-provoking titles
in the Speaker's Corner series

One Nation Under Guns
An Essay on an American Epidemic
Arnold Grossman

Two Wands, One Nation
An Essay on Race and Community in America
Richard D. Lamm

TABOR and Direct Democracy
An Essay on the End of the Republic
Bradley J. Young

God and Caesar in America
An Essay on Religion and Politics
Gary Hart

Ethics for a Finite World
An Essay Concerning a Sustainable Future
Herschel Elliott

Social Security and the Golden Age
An Essay on the New American Demographic
George McGovern

Think for Yourself!
An Essay on Cutting through the Babble, the Bias, and the Hype
Steve Hindes

The Enduring Wilderness
Protecting Our Natural Heritage through the Wilderness Act
Doug Scott

Parting Shots from My Brittle Bow
Reflections on American Politics and Life
Eugene J. McCarthy

The Brave New World of Health Care
What Every American Needs to Know about the Impending Health Care Crisis
Richard D. Lamm

For more information, visit our website, www.fulcrumbooks.com